MARRIAGES
are Made on Earth

Heather Jenner

DAVID & CHARLES
London   Newton Abbot   North Pomfret (Vt)

British Library Cataloguing in Publication Data

Jenner, Heather
   Marriages are made on earth.
1. Marriage — Great Britain — Public opinion —
   History — 20th century 2. Public opinion —
   Great Britain
   I. Title
   301.42'0941   HQ613

ISBN 0-7153-7662-4
Library of Congress Catalog Card Number: 78-74088

Printed in Great Britain
by Redwood Burn Limited, Trowbridge & Esher
for David & Charles (Publishers) Limited
Brunel House Newton Abbot Devon

Published in the United States of America
by David & Charles Inc
North Pomfret Vermont 05053 USA

Contents

1 Starting the Bureau

*Tips for girls in business. Pay more
attention to making up your minds
than your faces.*

B. C. FORBES

Mary Oliver and I — Mary was my partner for the first three years — watched with satisfaction as the signmaker hung up the wooden notice board: it looked good. When he had finished we climbed the stairs to the office that we had taken on the fifth floor of a building in New Bond Street, London. It was a scruffy little room for which we paid twenty-five shillings per week by the week. This rent included rates and the use of two chairs, two desks, a bookcase and a telephone. We thought that it needed cheering up so we bought buckets of yellow paint, and for several days clanked up and down Bond Street wearing old clothes and hoping that nobody we knew would see us. It was 1939, when things were not so informal, indeed tatty, as they are now and one dressed up to go to the West End.

We had chosen to have our office in Mayfair because it was the most glamorous and sought-after part of London. It was largely residential with gracious family houses, many of which were subsequently bombed and replaced by dull blocks. The few old houses that remain, except in an occasional mews, are now mostly business premises. Mayfair, as well as being a district, had given its name to a way of living. In the twenties there had been 'The Bright Young Things' who seemed to go in for practical jokes and gilded youth. In the thirties they had been succeeded by 'The Mayfair Set'. The Mayfair Set absorbed the Bright Young Things as older members. They were gilded less by birth than by money, and many of them courted publicity rather than avoided it as their predecessors had done. Some of their doings were reported in the gossip columns, but the more lurid stories went the rounds by word of mouth. Two beautiful and much publicised members 'doing' their first season as debs had had a bet as to which of the two would sleep with their hundredth man first. I always understood that the competition ended in a draw, but both contestants married well and in white, which was the desired end product of being presented and doing a season. The more money that was spent on a girl the more advantageous her marriage was expected to be. It was a very expensive marriage market.

In those days, too, in all strata of society parents were worried if their daughters remained single after the age of about twenty, but even girls in the rarified set of breeding, or money, or both, were beginning to rebel against this. They were demanding the right to as good an education as a boy, and after that the right to leave home, take a job, and choose their own friends. Families were smaller than they had been at the beginning of the century and family life was therefore more boring and constricting. Opportunities existed in the towns, or should have, but Britain was going through a severe economic crisis involving terrible unemployment, harsher in those days because neither the unions nor the social services were able to give enough help. This meant that any girl who had a visible means of support and could live with her family was discouraged from taking a job that a man trying to support a family could do.

Mary and I had observed this state of affairs from the Far East. I had been living in Ceylon (now Sri Lanka) where my father had been commanding the troops, and Mary had been staying in Assam. She had then travelled round India for a bit and come down to Ceylon to return home by the same boat on which I was travelling. We had never met before but had both been thinking along the same lines. We knew that our contemporaries who had been sitting about in

Britain were leading very dull lives and meeting few suitable men, whereas out in the Far East there were twenty eligible men to one woman and so many of them seemed to want wives. They used to say, 'When I go home I'm going to be married.' If you said, 'Congratulations. Who to?' they would say that they did not know but hoped that they would meet somebody. Most of them had about six months' leave, which did not give them a great deal of time to meet, woo and wed, so that they were often still bachelors when they returned. When we decided to start the Bureau we wrote and told several of them that they would be amongst our first clients: we also wrote to our girl friends and told them the same thing—we wanted a nucleus to work on, and we also wanted to practise interviewing. Some of them were annoyed, as people often are if you produce a really practical solution to their problems—but they were far more annoyed later when we did not use them.

Although we were both of us in our mid-twenties, optimistic and light-hearted, when we opened the Bureau we were deadly serious about what we wanted to do. We arrived back in England in March 1938. We knew that there was no marriage bureau operating in those days, but that there were newspapers which carried rather doubtful advertisements. In some cases the newspapers themselves invented the majority of the advertisements, which tended to be seductive to play the market; in others, agencies advertising under box numbers were doing the same thing.

We started in opposition to this, and, partly because we wanted all our clients to come and see us personally, we chose Bond Street in which to have our offices as it was easy to find and less confusing than the bigger streets such as Piccadilly, Regent Street or Oxford Street.

We decided to seek advice on how to do everything properly. We first went to a firm of well-known and established solicitors. We saw the junior partner, a correct and conventional man who was horrified at our proposals

9

and no help at all. It was obvious after a few minutes that we were getting nowhere, and the solicitor, really for something to say more than anything else, I think, asked us how much capital we had. Mary, who was by this time bored with him, looked at me and said, 'I don't know. How much is your beat worth?' That effectively finished the interview and we looked round for somebody more helpful and less stodgy.

I then remembered a friend of mine who was also a good solicitor but less old-fashioned. He saw the point of what we wanted to do at once. 'If you do this properly you have a good idea,' he said. He then took us to have Counsel's opinion on how to protect our clients and ourselves, and with his help we drew up the fundamental rules that we keep to this day. Chief amongst the rules are that we interview all our clients and that the interviews are free; we do not take on anybody unless they are free to marry which means that if they are getting a divorce they must have the decree absolute; we take on clients only if we think that we have a reasonable number of people to whom we can introduce them; we charge the same fee for everybody and the after-marriage fee is greater than the registration one; the initial fee entitles the client to introductions as and when we have them, unless we do not hear from them for one year; we never send out lists or photographs of clients and introductions are given one at a time. We also make it clear that we do not take up references. At the top of the form we have printed in large letters:

The purpose of the Marriage Bureau is to introduce with a view to marriage persons who desire to find matrimonial partners. Applicants are required to give full particulars of themselves and those particulars are then placed on the register of the Bureau. The more difficult the applicant's case the more limited the introductions will naturally be. The Bureau of course cannot do more than effect introductions nor hold itself responsible for the results and does not vouch for the correctness of the particulars passed on. These particulars should be verified by you. In the opinion of the Bureau it is essential for applicants to meet the relatives and friends of a potential husband or wife before they commit themselves to an engagement or marriage. If an applicant has any cause for suspicion or complaint he or she is asked to inform the Bureau immediately. The matter will of course be dealt with confidentially.

Next Mary went and asked the London County Council for a licence to start business. She came back with the vague impression that although they could not give us one, as far as they could see there was nothing to stop us starting. I would still like a licence.

All this took quite a long time. We had much to talk through between ourselves and we were also seeing our friends and enjoying life back in England, so it was not until April 1939 that we at last took the office. While we were painting it many of our friends came to see us.

Most of them were disapproving but fascinated; they seemed to think that we would end up behind bars for white-slave trafficking or some such thing. One, though, asked us how people were going to hear of us. 'We'll advertise,' we said cheerfully, not realising that it was going to be thirty years or so before the prestige papers which we wanted to be in would take us. 'Not good enough,' replied our friend. 'You must get publicity. Ring up the newspapers.' We did, in alphabetical order, and got through to the features editor every time — a thing that I have never been able to do since! The papers then were very large: it was between the Munich crisis and the war and the editors were looking for news other than war news. Most of them sent reporters round. Then Godfrey Winn, who in those days was writing for the *Sunday Express*, did his whole column about us.

11

Near the end of the week in which our pictures had been in every paper except the more sober ones, I thought that I should telephone my parents and tell them what I was doing. I had not told them what I was up to, nor had I used my father's name which was Lyon, but had chosen Jenner — a name that came from my mother's side of the family. I thought that it went better with Heather, and I also did not want to infuriate my father's mother who was a bit of a dragon. My parents only read the *Morning Post*, a very conventional paper, but I thought that the news of the venture would percolate through to them sometime. When I rang I hoped to get my mother as she was the least reactionary of the two, but my father answered. I took a deep breath and broke the news. To my amazement all he said was, 'Thank goodness somebody in the family is trying to make some money at last.' The next morning he came round to the office with a box of chocolates and some flowers. It was my mother who was in fact rather annoyed because I had used one of her names without asking her. Curiously enough it was about the only thing I ever did of which my grandmother approved; her generation, she pointed out, had had a dreadful time marrying off their daughters and it had cost them a great deal more than our fees.

Monday 17 April 1939 was our opening day. We both arrived in the office at 8.30 in the morning. I had put in the drawer of my desk *Bridge in Twenty Minutes* and a book on how to knit. I never got those twenty minutes nor can I knit. Thanks to all the publicity that we had had the previous week the postman had put so many letters through our box that we had difficulty in opening the door. When we did get in we sat down and, taking half each, opened the letters and put them into three piles — one men, one women, and one uncertain. While we were doing this there was a knock at the door. Mary answered it and came back looking startled. 'There's a man here,' she said. 'Let's toss for which of us will see him.' We did and I lost, so Mary took some letters out into the passage to open them there and I was left with our first client.

He was Major A., a retired Indian Army officer in his early forties. A kindly man and presumably a good leader of men, he took me through the interview rather than the other way about. To my horror he paid—the fee was five guineas to become a client and ten guineas if he or she got married through us—and I was left wondering what to do. He was too old for any of our girl friends, who would have looked upon him as middle-aged, so Mary and I applied ourselves to the letters again with a definite object in view— a wife for Major A. We thought that we would keep the money for a few days and then send it back if nobody suitable came along. Then another man arrived and I went out of the room with some letters while Mary interviewed him. He told her that several of his near relatives had 'handles to their names' and that any woman that he met must be in 'the book'. 'Does he mean the telephone book or *Debrett*'s, do you think?' Mary asked.

There was another small office on our landing which seemed to be empty, and it soon became obvious that we would need it. We also needed somebody to help us with the letters. Our original idea had been to answer them all by hand. As it happened, Mary couldn't spell and my hand-writing has always been difficult to read, so it was probably just as well that we changed our minds. We rang up our landlord about the other office, and the employment exchange for a secretary. The office we could have for one pound a week and the secretary's wages would be three. We also needed a typewriter. I had managed to produce fifty pounds' capital and we held ten guineas in fees. I went off to Harrods where I had an account and bought a typewriter on the 'never-never'. Coming back I found to my joy that Mary had interviewed two women and although neither of them was suitable for our two men—one was a shorthand typist and the other a shop assistant from Oxford Street, both young — it at least showed that there were women about who wanted to get married too. Mary had also engaged a secretary whom she described as perfect. 'Wait till you see her,' she said. 'She had a good reference, too. I spoke to her former employer over the telephone.'

It was my turn to interview next and I got Rosemary. She was twenty-two, an ex-deb of, I guessed, fairly conservative behaviour. Her father was a distinguished professional man who had been knighted. Perfect for Mary's 'handle' man, I thought. She was a pretty girl, a bit on the plump side, and wore expensive but unremarkable clothes — handmade shoes, a well-cut coat and skirt and a necklace of small pearls. She had well-kept hands with buffed rather than painted nails, no eye make-up and a discreet pink lipstick. She lived at home, had an allowance from Daddy and wanted to meet a man a few years older than she was, possibly in the army (naturally a good regiment) because she would like to live abroad. I could imagine her in some pleasant hill station in India wearing a regimental brooch of small diamonds to back up the pearls and talking about all the right things to all the right people. If Mary's client wasn't suitable, there was nobody amongst my friend but I thought that possibly she might do for a polo-playing acquaintance from Colombo whom we had put on the books and who was coming home soon; or perhaps Mary had some friend from India who might suit. By the end of the day we had sent out forms to a hundred people.

The next day the perfect secretary arrived. She had grey hair parted down the middle and drawn back into a neat bun; she looked respectable and tidy and seemed motherly and efficient sorting out the letters, and she typed like lightning.

By Friday we had interviewed some fifty clients and collected about two hundred pounds. We realised that we would have to return some of the money, but we had made a number of appointments for the next few weeks so thought that we would keep the money for the time being and see how the introductions went. We did not like to hurt people's feelings and were diffident about saying that we could not help them, so our plan was to return the money with a tactful letter, to the people that we could not take on, rather than tell them to their face. Meanwhile we did not want to leave the cash in the office over the weekend. We had thought small rather than big about the business and the results of our publicity had caught us by surprise, so much so that we had not even opened a bank account.

I set out to remedy this: putting the money into a paper bag I went into the first bank I saw, emptied the notes on to the counter, and said to the man behind it that I would like to open a business account. He looked rather surprised and said that I ought to see the manager. A few minutes later he showed me into an office in which there was a cherubic-looking man who smiled at me benignly. I sat down and told him about the business and that we'd probably be returning most of the money we had taken. He said that would be quite all right but that if the business really got going we should become a company which would mean we would need an accountant. We took this piece of advice and several others that he gave us at other times and he became a father figure to us until he retired. It was only years later after Stephen Potter and I were married that I found out that he had not only been Stephen's bank manager but his uncle as well, so he was quite used to eccentricities in his clients.

For the first few months we really worked. As there was nobody to teach us, we had to think everything out for ourselves and could not teach anybody else until we had learnt by trial and error. We seldom left the office until late at night, never had time to get to a hairdresser or dress-maker, and lived on fishcakes from a restaurant below us. They were less fattening, we thought, than sandwiches and easy to eat cold in one hand as we answered the telephone or wrote out introductions. One journalist who came to see us went back to Fleet Street and told somebody that we seemed nice girls but looked very peculiar.

It seemed to us looking out of the office window to be an exceptionally sunny summer. At weekends we used sometimes to take the matching up, or the mating as we called it, to one of the parks. What people thought we were doing I cannot imagine. We used to take the clients' cards along in tin boxes and argue hotly with each other as to whether Mary's Mr X. was nice enough for my Miss Y. We learnt soon that you could become very interested in and possessive about your clients, to the point of being competitive in doing your best for them. We sent back some of the fees that we had taken during the first two or three weeks, but were able to give suitable introductions to Major A., the 'handle' man, Rosemary, and the two girls whom Mary had interviewed.

The perfect secretary worked steadily, too, but her appearance seemed to change; for the better we thought, when she started using make-up which suited her, but weekly it grew brighter, eventually becoming garish. At the same time her hair started to change colour. It went from grey to brown, from there to chestnut, and then to carrot red. Until the chestnut stage it had still been done in a neat bun, but between then and the final carrot stage she had had it cut off and permed. She had certainly changed her image but we were not sure that we liked the new one. To begin with we had been pleased because we thought that she enjoyed her job and that it was doing her good; later we didn't like to criticise because we thought that it would be impertinent. If she had been our own age we would have been bolder; as it was we hoped that it didn't seem as bad to other people as it looked to us.

One morning a very rich client of ours from the Midlands rang us and said that he had a serious complaint to make.

Could we meet him for a drink after work that evening? He then told us that a woman whose name we did not recognise had said that his name and particulars had been given to her by us. She had written a very good letter and they arranged to meet. He was in his late forties and wanted to meet a woman in her late thirties or early forties. The woman whom he met, he said, was fifty-five if she was a day, over-made-up, wore black net stockings and tarty shoes, and had improbably red hair. He added that he had seen her a few weeks before walking down our stairs carrying a pile of letters. He was very nice about it, fortunately, and understood how it had happened.

Mary and I decided that our 'perfect secretary' would have to go, but which of us was to tell her? Mary wanted to toss for it, but I refused and we agreed that it would have to be a joint effort. It was painful but not difficult. She knew that she had been caught red-handed and left immediately.

We replaced her by Miss B. who really was perfect. She came to us as a junior — she was just sixteen — but her typing was as good as her predecessor's had been. She had the most extraordinary filing system, but could produce anything that we wanted in a matter of seconds, and she seemed instinctively to know who and who not to put through to us on the telephone. She stayed with us as a full-blown secretary until she was called up to work in a ministry in the war. There she was so bored, with so little work to do and so much time in which to do it, that she used to come up and type letters for us in her lunch hour.

Another excitement was moving into our next office. By about June we felt that we should get somebody to help us with the interviewing and that we were experienced enough to teach them the wrinkles. This meant that again we needed more room. Fortunately, there was an office to let just up the street. The tenants were leaving London because of the threat of approaching war and offered us the few remaining months of the lease, saying that the landlord would surely be reasonable if we were to renew it afterwards. Our solicitor said that we were taking a bit of a chance, but thought that it might be all right; he advised us to spend the minimum of money on anything so that we could move out quickly if necessary. But we became over-confident and bought some rather nice curtains and carpets, only to find that the landlord was indeed being unreasonable. He wanted us to take the office on a seven-year lease at a much higher rent.

'What shall we do?' I wailed to our long-suffering solicitor. 'We've only three weeks to go.' He advised us to sit tight until we had found somewhere else. For some reason the lease was in my name so, as he put it, 'If they put the bailiffs on to you it should be easy for you to avoid them as it is only you they are out to catch.'

There were two doors to the office and a fire escape, and twice I managed to evade a bailiff just in time. After three weeks of living in a state of siege we at last found another office. Greatly relieved at the prospect of signing the lease in a few days, we settled down, after our two staff had left, to finish off the mating for the day, and we did not lock the door as we had been doing. Then the door opened and a man said, 'Miss Jenner?' Without thinking I looked up from my work and said 'yes', whereupon he handed me the writ. I asked him to sit down so that he could tell me what I was meant to do next and he chose a swivel chair which we had just bought second-hand. As he leant back in it something snapped and he went over backwards. Luckily he wasn't hurt and had no hard feelings. The next week we signed the lease for an office on the second floor of 124 New Bond Street where we have been ever since. For this we paid the princely sum of £35 4s 11d per quarter. Now we pay £500.

From the first it was evident that far from our clients' being similar to our own friends and contemporaries they represented a cross-section of society. One newspaper interview quoted us as saying that our clients ranged from plumbers to peers and from charladies to countesses, which was a rough statement of fact. Amongst our first five hundred clients on the men's side we did have a plumber and a peer. We had an MP, professional men, businessmen, farmers, landowners, members of the forces, and, rather more unusually, a maker of artificial limbs and a nib maker. We also had a special constable whose chief occupation once the blitz had started seemed to be to get the prostitutes off the streets before the bombing began. If they got back to their flats before he caught them they could not be prosecuted. He used to come in and have cups of tea with us between chases. I don't think he ever caught one and I do remember that he told us that one girl turned her ankle when she was running away from him so he helped her home.

Our women clients did not have the same variety of jobs as the men. Most of the younger ones lived at home with their parents. We did have a charwoman, the widow of an earl, and the daughter of another earl. We had ex-debs, models, beauticians, secretaries, shop assistants, dress and hat shop owners, nurses, nannies, teachers and matrons. We also had a well-known actress, an Eton dame, a lady surgeon, and a lady dentist.

One of our richest clients was a contractor in New York — a tremendous anglophile; another very rich one was the businessman from the Midlands who had met our 'perfect secretary'. But it was possible at that time to live well on what now seems to us to be very little money. One man spent most of the year in Le Touquet playing golf on £700 a year; another lived in Scotland and had fishing and shooting on £1000 per annum. A smallholder in Cornwall lived on £3 15s a week — he owned his own house and considered himself quite comfortable, thank you.

Mary had interviewed the MP who was one of our most tricky customers and noted for raising questions in the House. She felt sure that he intended to raise one about the

Marriage Bureau, although at the same time she thought that he was genuine about wanting to get married. We were convinced that if we got him married we would never hear any more from him. He asked to meet somebody considerably younger than himself and after a few introductions, to his surprise, we introduced him to his dream girl to whom he proposed. Unfortunately for him she turned him down—she found him too dictatorial and set in his ways.

Many of the girls were only earning £1 to 30s a week—one girl who was working outside London earned 17s a week and another 15s, but both lived in. Our own invaluable Miss B. began at 30s a week but rose quickly to the heights of £3, and as she lived at home she thought that she was well off. The lady dentist aged twenty-six earned £550 and the lady surgeon £800. We found it difficult to get men to meet these last two, partly because the men thought that after a long training such women would want to stay at work rather than run a house, which was then the usual thing for a middle-class married woman to do, and partly because their particular professions gave men an unreasonable feeling of distaste. Whereas a male surgeon is likely to be a romantic figure, saving lives with great coolness, the image did not seem to apply to female surgeons. One man who met the lady surgeon said, 'When I looked at those delicate hands I thought of them cutting people open.' One girl of twenty-seven, who had a private income of £1,500 a year, was very suspicious that she would be married only for her money. We did not divulge her income nor that of other women with money. An heiress, whose name was that of a well-known product, at our suggestion used another name for the purpose of meeting people through us.

After a month or so we had learnt a great deal about interviewing. We never flinched when some good lady from the shires brayed at us that she had 'never expected to come to a place like this'. We realised that it was just a reflex nervous reaction. Nor did we get upset if a man looked us straight in the eye and said that he didn't like girls who wore make-up and long painted fingernails.

It was more difficult to give a good interview then than it is now. People were not so used to talking about themselves, their hopes and their feelings, and they did not like filling in forms. We only dared have sixteen questions, and one was 'What is your name?' and another 'What is your address?' Now we have forms with some sixty questions on them, to be answered, not just ticked. Rather than listing, for example, blonde, brunette, redhead, grey-haired, we ask them the colour of their hair, and as a reminder to ourselves we make any necessary remarks such as 'beautiful colour', 'tinted', 'well cut' on the form after the interview. The shorter forms meant that we had little guide to the sort of life that the clients led and the sort of life that they wanted to lead after they were married, nor did we get the same amount of information about their educational standards, ambitions and background as we do now.

We learnt to be interested and never surprised and not to give clients false hope in an attempt to be kind. It was a great help in this simply to apply the rule of supply and demand. Taking an extreme hypothetical case, if a man of ninety asked us to introduce him to a girl of twenty-one, we would say with perfect truth that we had not got a girl of twenty-one who wanted to marry a man of ninety at the moment. This same approach covers a multitude of cases from sad ones to 'try-ons'. It is difficult to turn down some of the pleasant and attractive older women who come to us, but the unfortunate fact is that there are fewer older men than older women in existence. A woman who has been married a number of years has often relied on her husband for her social life—particularly if she has not had a career and has occupied herself with her home and children. If she is left on her own she may be too diffident to get her social life going again and often does not have enough money to do so. A man left on his own can more easily invite a woman out to dinner or a theatre than a similarly placed woman can invite a man, and he can ask someone from any age group. Also, because he is in short supply, a man is at a premium: hostesses need him to make up numbers, and women on their own would like him as an occasional escort. Other people whom we have to turn down sometimes are those with bad physical infirmities. We help them when we can and ask clients who otherwise would be suitable if they would meet them. In all cases we say that we have nobody at the moment, but will let them know when we have.

In the early days we both got caught in the 'guess my age' game. Mary told a woman in her forties that she thought she was fifty—later she told me that she had thought she was sixty—and the woman flounced out of the office. Just after that I was asked by a man how old he was. I thought about fifty but over-reacted after Mary's experience and told him late thirties. He was equally furious because he took a pride in being a grand old man and liked everybody to know his age, nearly sixty, so that he would be congratulated on being so healthy and active. He said that I was obviously no judge of anything at all and it took me about ten minutes persuasive talking to convince him that I had been misled by his suntan and his vigorous manner.

We also fell into the trap of taking on clients through a well-intentioned friend or relation. The first time we did this was when Lady Y., who was a friend of mine and had been a famous beauty, wanted to help a girl whom she knew wanted to get married but who didn't seem to meet the right people. The girl was shy and Lady Y. was certain that nothing would induce her to come to the Marriage Bureau. She filled in a form for the girl and described the sort of person whom she thought she would like to marry—she said that she had asked the girl lots of questions about this. I was then to explain the situation to any man who might be suitable and ask him to get in touch with Lady Y. It didn't work: they all loved Lady Y., but ignored the tongue-tied girl who was amazed by all these new acquaintances. Several mothers and fathers tried the same sort of thing, but it worked only once and then after numerous complications; the father had to admit what he had done and the girl nearly called the wedding off because she thought the arrangement too contrived. After that if a parent ever came in with his or her child we always insisted that we interviewed the child alone. As often as not we found that he or she was in love with somebody of whom their parents did not approve and we had to tell the parents that we did not think their child really wanted to get married through us at the moment.

We did not get many people who were divorced as divorce was not as prevalent then as it is now. In 1940 in Britain there were 6,915 divorces and in 1977 113,500. There was still a social stigma attached to having been 'through the courts'. It could cost a man his job and career and a woman her reputation.

We had difficulty in finding introductions for Lady P. because she had run away from an elderly husband who had subsequently divorced her. Major A. who met and liked her said that he was prepared to bet that she'd never remarry unless we produced somebody else with a title, preferably a better one. The 'handle' man met her too but she thought him dull; there were not many others whom she could meet.

We were having our successes though. Rosemary got engaged to a man in the navy who played polo, and Major A. married one of the women from the shires. Our rich Birmingham man married a woman almost as rich as himself—they were both quiet and unassuming and had asked that their incomes should not be divulged. Our smallholder in Cornwall married a woman who had left Devonshire to work in London and longed to get back to the West Country. He was a widower of fifty-six with a boy of twelve, born to him and his wife after nine years of marriage. When he remarried in 1939 he wrote, 'My wife has made us very comfortable, it is wonderful what a difference a woman makes about the house, and my little boy is very fond of her.' In 1964 he wrote me another letter saying:

> We have been married twenty-four years and I shall be eighty in September. We have been thinking about you lately because we saw an article about you in the Daily Press. If you should happen to be down in this part of the country we hope that you will look us up, and we will give you a hearty welcome. We have been very happy.

His marriage had been speeded up as had many others because of the feeling of approaching war. When it was announced Mary and I had gone down to the Hamble for a 'last' weekend's sailing on a friend's yacht. At 'Stand by for an important announcement' we sat down feeling weak at the knees. If anybody had told me then that I should still be running the Marriage Bureau today I would have thought that they were mad — it seemed like the end of the world.

2 Sex

What is it men in women do require?
The Lineaments of Gratified Desire.
What is it women do in men require?
The Lineaments of Gratified Desire.

WILLIAM BLAKE

Although a happy sex life is one of the chief ingredients in a good marriage, from the beginning of Queen Victoria's reign until the middle of this century sex was rarely talked about in polite society, even between mother and daughter. So much was it a closed book that there were stories of many nineteenth-century brides who had tried to throw themselves out of the window or fainted dead away on their wedding night when confronted with their bridegroom and the facts of life. In the thirties brides were unlikely to do this, but love to most of them was equated with romance rather than sex.

My own generation had little sex education. At school we had biology lessons which did not hold my attention as we never progressed beyond flowers and pollen. On the evening before I left, the headmistress asked me if I knew what was 'worse than death'. I assumed she meant rape and didn't feel prepared to discuss it with her so I mumbled 'yes'.

Luckily from the age of eight I went to a boarding school in Devonshire which was near the kennels of the local hunt, and the woman who taught me riding was the girl friend of the huntsman. I learnt to take a keen interest in the breeding of hounds, and talked freely about coming on heat and periods of gestation. Many of my fellow-pupils came from farming families and under their influence my interest turned to horses and cows. Soon I could hold forth about slipping foals, mastitis and contagious abortion, but strangely enough I related none of this to humans until I went to my public school where I heard surprising stories about men and women which vaguely seemed to have something in common with the facts I knew of in animals. After much thought, and reading *Lady Chatterly's Lover* under the bedclothes by torchlight, I got a fairly clear picture of what probably happened.

By the time I was an adult the term 'sex appeal' had come into fashion, but was applied mostly to film stars playing sirens or to dream men, rather than to respectable men and women. Love scenes in films and plays were not as informative as they are now, and were sometimes so played down that at the end of the story when the hero and heroine were going to be married the audience had never even seen them kiss. In very daring films if a couple ever got to bed the man always (by the law of that time) had to have one foot on the ground. Even in this strange position the camera was only on them for a second or two. No pornographic films were shown in public and books were strictly censored. It was not legal to sell the unexpurgated edition of *Lady Chatterly's Lover* until after the famous trial about the book in 1960.

From the point of view of the Marriage Bureau, this meant that we had very little if any discussion about sex with our clients. They would tell us the sort of person that they found attractive, but little about themselves otherwise. I always politely assumed that every unmarried girl was a virgin, and that most unmarried men were not. If when I had interviewed Rosemary — the ex-deb who had been one of my first clients — I had asked her in a roundabout way whether she had had an affair, she would probably have lied.

Traditionally, women had been brought up to believe that their virginity was a prize that they kept to give away on their wedding night. It could be a good bargaining point for a woman. If she had attracted a man she could withhold her favours until he made her his bride. This was particularly important if he was a good catch and it was the only way that she could get him to marry her. It could be difficult for her of course if she had not behaved as chastely as she had led her bridegroom to believe. This problem was not new. Muriel Segal in her book *Virgins* describes how expertly the girls in ancient Troy dealt with such a dilemma. As worshippers of a river goddess, on the eve of their wedding night they used to slide down the rocky banks into the river, splash about in the cold water for twenty minutes or so, and then climb back up the hill to the temple of the goddess and say, 'Now I have sacrificed my virginity.' Girls in the twentieth century used much the same methods, but put their loss down to skiing or riding or playing strenuous games.

Rosemary and her contemporaries were living when there was one law for men and another for women for many things, but particularly for sex. Men could go to a chemist and buy contraceptives, whereas an unmarried woman had the greatest difficulty, even at the new birth-control centres, in obtaining them. Abortions were illegal, expensive and dangerous. Women with money who 'got into trouble' could probably get out of it if they paid enough. Sometimes they simply retired from the social scene for a few months. Shotgun weddings were common and a remarkable number of 'premature' babies were hearty, heavy and bouncing.

Men were conditioned to thinking that most girls did not sleep around. They did not take it for granted that any girl who flirted with them was prepared to go to bed. If she did they felt they were lucky, but possibly thought that it had all been too easy. Girls were much more protected by their families too. Parents met the young men who called for their daughters, and some of them waited up for them until they returned. They wanted to know in the first place where they were going and when they came back where they had been.

Some well-brought up girls behaved like the legendary

Victorian Miss. Elsie was one of these. An anaemic-looking English rose who could have done with more make-up and prettier clothes, she told me that she had never been out with any man except her brother. He had now met a girl with whom he was going steady so he had sent her along to see us. She told me that when her brother had introduced her to a man she had always left him to do all the talking, so none of them had ever asked her out. When I asked her if she would have accepted if they had, she said that she wasn't sure.

I took her on with some misgiving, but thought that as she had come to see us she was prepared to make an effort to overcome her shyness.

Of course, the first thing that happened was that a very respectable and dull young man I had asked to meet her gave her what he described as a friendly peck on the cheek when he saw her home and she slapped his face. He was amazed and thought it quite funny, but she looked upon the incident as something on a par with rape and rushed into the office the next day in a panic.

I privately thought that it was wonderful that he had actually taken her out, let alone given her a chaste kiss, and tried to calm her down and persuade her that it was a conventional way of saying farewell. She was not placated, but luckily she joined the ATS not long afterwards which brought her much more up to date with contemporary thought. She forgave us, came to see us again, and eventually married through us towards the end of the war.

Elsie's type of girl was a dying race, but there were still some left who had been brought up to believe that all men were lecherous monsters and that friendship between the sexes was impossible. The war taught them otherwise. They worked side by side with men and enjoyed a camaraderie that they had never dreamt of, and a few men discovered that it was the women who could be lecherous.

After the war men and women had a much more natural

relationship together; men became less chivalrous and women less servile. Women felt that they had earned the right to have the same advantages and freedoms as men and they took them. Many of them did not go home to their families when they were demobilised; they became independent — bachelor girls rather than spinsters. Their sex lives became their own business. The ban on selling contraceptives to unmarried women had been lifted so that there was less risk; they had also been improved. Later, abortions were legalised.

By the fifties talk about sex was much more frank; the media had started to take it up. The *Sunday Graphic* had a headline running 'What do you look for in a husband? 1. A lover 2. A friend and 3. A provider.' The teenage idols changed too from smiling and cuddly — almost cosy — to cool and sexy, even mean and moody. A psychiatrist explained this as being a protection against sex. The 'come hither' look which had formerly been treated with caution was now taken literally; the mean and moody one meant that you had to be wooed.

By the sixties the Pill had been invented and abortions legalised under certain conditions. These aids led to more freedom in sex, as the media continued to spread the good news. Everybody was told that they could and should enjoy sex, and how to do so. Some of the things that were published or seen on the screen were ugly and distasteful, but much was informative and brought the subject of sex into the open so that it was discussed, and men and women had more knowledge and less guilt.

By this time our clients were more willing to talk to us about themselves and we added more questions to our forms. One of them was 'Have you ever been engaged before?' To this both men and women will say such things as, 'No I haven't but I've lived with someone.' One girl said, 'Not engaged, but two common-law marriages, one lasted six months and the other two.' She had no feeling of security she said; she now wanted to be married in a church and thought marriage should be a sacrament. A man said that he had lived with a girl for five years. She had seemed so independent that he did not feel she needed him; he now felt that he would like the responsibility of being a husband and father. If they reply that they have not been engaged before we ask them if they have had any friends and affairs. There is no conventional reason for them to lie now and if they say that they have not we are prepared to believe them.

Janet was twenty-three years old — well-cut sleek black hair, good skin, large dark eyes, well dressed and very composed. She said that she had never been engaged before. When we questioned her further she said, 'I'm very old fashioned. I have high moral standards, I don't want to sleep around and I have no intention of doing so.' Unlike Elsie she liked men and liked to make friends with them, but she had not met one whom she would like to marry. She took her time with us; the men she met liked and admired her and one went as far as proposing, but she turned him down. We began to wonder if she was frigid, although her looks belied this. Eventually she got engaged and is now happily married.

A girl like Janet is admired by many men. Men, however, are more likely to come under suspicion if they say that they have never had a relationship with a girl. Because of the old tradition that they were permitted to have affairs, they are not credited with fine feelings or moral sense but rather suspected of being undersexed or homosexual. The few who say that they have not had affairs, unless they are very young, say that they have not done so on moral grounds.

In my office my interviewers and I discussed the types of girls who slept around and those who did not. Those who were very ambitious, particularly if they had to put in long hours of study to achieve their objective, tended not to. This applied to men too. They might have an affair with somebody, but if they were not prepared to marry that person they would keep the affair very much second to their work.

One interviewer said about the girls, 'You can tell, I think. I might be wrong but it's a sort of attitude. The girl who comes in, wants children, doesn't want to work after marriage, at any rate not while the children are young, and is quite prepared to meet a boy who hasn't a very high salary, I think that you can say that if she is not a virgin she has had a serious affair, but that is about all. The girls who come in and say that they want a man with a substantial income have been sleeping around. They are usually more flamboyant than the others and have been used to having a good time. They want security but don't want to settle for a humdrum life.'

When we first started the Bureau I do not think that many of the clients — particularly the younger ones — slept together before they married. Now I would think that a lot of them do. But since many of the girls who come to us complain that the men they meet casually just want to go to bed with them, they are not likely to pay our fees to sleep with a marriage bureau client unless they have decided that they want to marry.

The younger generation, too, seem in general to be more sensible about sex than their elders. One of our elderly men wrote to us to say that he must be married by the next winter because he had booked a double cabin on a cruise — it was cheaper to get one with a bath that way, he explained. When we told him that we could not guarantee anything he joined all the same, but was so anxious about the double cabin that he always mentioned it on the first meeting, which was hardly calculated to make a woman feel that she would be loved for herself alone! Leaving it to the last possible moment he cancelled the double cabin and bath in favour of a single and a shower and we never heard from him again.

One very pretty woman in her fifties behaved as she had

probably done in the 1940s before her first marriage. She asked one or two of our clients whom she met and liked down to stay with her and, as one put it, 'beckoned me up the stairs, practically stair by stair and then rushed into her bedroom and locked and bolted the door'.

We seldom hear such stories from younger people. Sometimes they may say that they went on holiday together, very occasionally they will say that it didn't work out, but usually it does and they get engaged. They do not seem to have the same will-you-won't-you problems as some of the older generation have.

Older people too have a disparity of views, especially the women. Penny, in her mid-forties, ebullient and looking younger, ticked me off because I said that it would be difficult to get men younger than herself to meet her. She explained that she was highly sexed and didn't want to meet a man older than herself because he wouldn't be able to cope.

Mrs Y., who was the same age but looked much older, and anything but ebullient, said to my interviewer, 'The older the better you know, dear. If they're quite old they won't want it, will they?' She had been married and had had children and I can only imagine that she had no pleasure out of sex.

Many women haven't. Mrs X., a pretty and beautifully dressed woman in her mid-thirties, told me that although she and her husband had had children and slept together regularly she had never had an orgasm until she took a lover.

Madame G., a bubbling and vivacious French woman, said, 'You have to dominate an Englishman and tell him how he can please you. English women are too shy and reserved, they don't tell their men what to do. All the best lovers are trained by French women.' When I asked her why then were French men so notoriously unfaithful to their wives she brushed the question aside saying that they had to live up their reputation.

Major P. came to see us. Good looking, well set up, and glowing with health, he told us that he was fifty-five and kept assuring us of his virility. We were quite prepared to believe him, but advised him that we could not promise to find him girls in their thirties, women in their forties would be more likely. At this he complained that they would be just about to start the menopause and would be moody, temperamental and frigid.

One man in his sixties whose passion was travelling in Italy and studying its pictures and architecture said that he wanted to meet a woman who, if possible, had the same tastes, must speak Italian and drive a car. She must also have got over the menopause. At the time I had on my books a half-Italian woman who would be perfect for him I thought. I told her about Mr P. and the menopause and she roared with laughter. 'I don't have those problems,' she said. 'I just have pills, my only problem is they make me fat.'

Suzanne who was fifty-five said it was all nonsense; she had had the menopause and was as interested in sex as ever. It was men in their fifties and sixties who often had worries.

This can be true but some men remain potent very late in life. The Duc de Richelieu, born at the end of the seventeenth century, a premature seven-months' baby, married his third wife just before his eighty-fourth birthday. She was a woman of forty, four years younger than his son and heir. They were married in February 1780 and the ceremony was followed by a ball. By April the duchess was pregnant, but had a miscarriage. Later there was a rumour that she was pregnant again and the queen of France asked the duke if it was true. His reply was, 'I think not, Madame, unless it is as a result of last night.' Then, after a pause, 'Or this morning.'

We have never had anybody as optimistic as the Duc de Richelieu, but we do get strange requests from time to time. Recently, a man in his seventies who has a great deal of money and lives abroad for several months of the year said that all the women he met there were in their twenties. Further questioning revealed that he stayed in very expensive hotels and went to fashionable bars frequented by these young ladies. He wanted us to find him somebody in the same age group as he would like a permanent relationship with one of them which would lead to marriage.

Another man in his seventies whom we could not help was a fishmonger whose young wife had run off and left him with two children. He had divorced her but, undeterred by this bad experience, he wanted another young wife and more children. His wife was not to be over thirty and was not only to look after their family, however large it became, but also to help in the shop.

One would-be client we had to disappoint was a woman of sixty who said that she wanted to meet a man of thirty because a man in her own age group could not satisfy her sexually. We have some men who will meet women up to about ten years older than themselves—they are usually under forty—but very few who will go up higher than that, and the ones that are prepared to we have suspected of being undersexed and looking for a mother figure. The woman coming to the Marriage Bureau for a husband, however, does not want that sort of role.

I think that people often make too much fuss about age; so much depends on the person, their health and their personality. Some people are never young and some never old.

In the Duc de Richelieu's day society talked about sex freely and we are now doing so again. People who have problems can get help, and more and more are doing so.

Not long ago a beautifully dressed and sophisticated woman came into the office. 'I want to talk about sex,' she said. The interviewer who opened the door was a bit surprised at such a direct approach and to gain time said, 'Are you one of our clients?' To which the woman replied,

'No. Have I come to the wrong place? My husband says we need advice.' She was quite unabashed when we told her that she had and gave her the address of the Marriage Guidance Council.

We do not give advice on sexual matters because we are not qualified to do so, but our clients—particularly those who have come to us after a broken marriage—tell us about their problems. One woman told me that she was so frightened of having a baby if she married that she had had herself sterilised. Several men told us that they had had vasectomies. One had had a wife who only wanted to have one child at most and had been advised by her doctor not to take the Pill. After the second child was born her husband suggested that she should be sterilised. She asked him how he was going to cope with the babies while she was in hospital, so it was decided that he should have a vasectomy. She died a few years later and he now wanted to marry again. He said that he would have liked another child of his own, and in fact married a woman with a young baby whom he looked upon as his.

Another man who had had a vasectomy came to us after an unfortunate experience. He had been in love with a woman who had children and did not want any more. She insisted that she would not marry him unless he had the operation. He did, but she married somebody else.

One or two divorced women told us that their husbands had been impotent; and divorced men sometimes said that their wives had been frigid. The most common complaint from both husband and wife was that they had had thoroughly enjoyable affairs before marriage, but afterwards they had found their sex life dull.

Suzie, in her mid-thirties, who had been a model and still had a wonderful figure and looks, told me that before she and her husband married they had had tremendous fun. He often called on her instead of going to a business lunch or even to his office, and stayed on well into the afternoon. On

Saturdays they would lie in bed watching the racing on TV. 'We often missed the big race,' she said.

After they married all was changed. He went to his office from nine until six, and sometimes had a drink with 'old so-and-so' on the way home: 'It was good to keep in with him, he was useful.' On Saturdays, if they watched the racing, they sat in different armchairs. But regularly every Saturday night he wanted to make love to her. When she asked him why he had changed, he was surprised and explained that they were together now for ever, so there was no need for clandestine meetings, nor, she presumed, for missing the big race. That was when she decided to take a lover and their marriage broke up.

A man told me the same sort of story, from his point of view. He had had an affair with a woman and had married her chiefly because she was sexually attractive to him. I asked him what went wrong, and whether she had changed after marriage and not enjoyed sex so much. 'No,' he replied severely, 'she complained that I did not make love to her enough, and said that love-making was what marriage was for.' I replied that she probably thought that love-making was an important part of marriage, whereupon he stormed out of the office shouting, 'You women are all the same.'

Undoubtedly there is often a change of feeling once a couple are married. When they are courting there is a feeling of expectation, of a special occasion when they meet, and they mostly see each other at their best. Most sensible people realise this and think in terms of building up a deeper relationship, together with sex. Once married, expectation can if necessary be created in other ways, particularly if the couple have friends, a good social life, and plenty to do. A special treat, an unexpected present, or a nice surprise will help. Such things, together with an understanding of each other's sexual needs can all contribute to the building of a satisfactory love life after marriage.

There is a saying in France that when a woman is no longer aware of the warmth of her husband's body, but only conscious of its weight, she is tired of him sexually. Another saying is that if everything is all right in bed the rest of the marriage will be all right too. I would not go as far as that, but would say that a good sex life is one of the strongest bonds in a happy marriage.

3 The Permissive Age

I asked a thief to steal me a peach:
He turned up his eyes.
I ask'd a lithe lady to lie her down:
Holy and meek she cries.

As soon as I went an angel came;
He wink'd at the thief
And smil'd at the dame,
And without one word spoke
Had a peach from the tree,
And twix't earnest and joke
Enjoy'd the Lady.

WILLIAM BLAKE

The 'Permissive Age' grew out of 'Swinging London', safer and easier abortion, and a newer and controversial contraceptive—the Pill.

I heard about the Pill in very early days, when the first experiments were being made. One of my clients had had a problem with facial hair and had been sent to a specialist who asked her if she was thinking of getting married in the near future. She said that she wasn't—this was before she came to me—but the question made her curious. She became much more so when she saw that the bottle of pills that she had been given had no medical formula on it. She gave a tablet to a chemist friend of hers to analyse and he told her it was a contraceptive pill. By the time she came to see me she had successfully got rid of the hair on her face, and she later married and had children. As this was over twenty years ago I presume the pills were a less sophisticated version of the ones taken now.

Its very name made the Permissive Age sound very light-hearted and emancipated. No guilt, no responsibilities, just fun—and devil take the hindmost. New words like unisex and wife-swapping came in. I was in the United States when wife-swapping became the talk of the day. On a phone-in programme I was asked what I thought of it. I replied that if I understood it correctly it meant that if my husband took a fancy to a lady I would be expected to have an affair with her husband, and that I would prefer to choose my own lover. This was obviously not the answer expected of me and the compère smoothed it over by saying that I was giving the sophisticated European point of view. This was not so. My reply was off the cuff, but I had lived in small self-contained communities where my father had been stationed. There had been only army people, and rumours and small scandals floated round—Major so-and-so was in love with Captain so-and-so's wife, and so it went on. As long as everybody kept to the rules of the game real scandals were avoided. Sometimes an officer was hurriedly posted to another part of the country, and I did know of one couple who did a real swap and married each other's husband and wife.

Ann Leslie, writing in the *Daily Mail* about the sexual revolution in the United States in 1976, made it sound as if many American women agreed with me. She wrote that wives were not easily swapped by their chauvinist husbands, and that husbands were cheating and taking hookers along instead. The wives seemed to be losing out.

Adolscents have not found the new mood so ideal either. There seem to be fewer rules and no clear guidance. Even those of eighteen or over, who have reached the age of majority, and certainly those of sixteen, who are at the age of consent, find this new freedom a problem, and are often perplexed and anxious. Their friends boast about the affairs they have had—probably exaggerating—and accuse them of being undersexed or prudish if they do not have them too. Parents in their anxiety sometimes make things worse.

Several girls have said that their mothers told them to go to the doctor and ask for the Pill, when in fact there was no need—nobody had tried to sleep with them. This made them feel more inadequate than ever.

The Press, which can be so helpful, sometimes added to the confusion. In the Monday issue of one well-known newspaper with an enormous circulation the message of the two middle pages was clear. Across a drawing of a voluptuous-looking young matron wearing a scanty bra, the briefest of pants, and a belt with a dagger in it, was written in two-inch-high letters THE HUNTRESS. The minor headlines were provocative: 'Our marriage is fine now I have taken a lover'; 'I need more loving than he can give me'; and 'Now I'm the one to say "when"'. The first two quotes were from women with children. All three women said that they loved their husbands, although they took numerous lovers, and would not break up their marriages. It was frank talk and there was no harm in it for adults: they could approve or disapprove as they wished. But four pages back in the paper was an advice column. Presumably to make the paper a family one it published two letters from fourteen-year-olds. A girl wrote, 'My Mum is my problem.' Not, as one might have expected from the eye-catching middle pages, because she had been found in bed with a different lover every day, but because she did not like her daughter going out with friends in the evenings, and insisted, if she did go out she had to be back by 9.30 p.m.

The advice given to the girl by a well-known woman writer answering the problem was conventional, but I couldn't help feeling that the youngsters going through the paper to see if their letters had been printed must have seen the middle pages and wondered if that was how their mothers behaved, and if so, just how much they should take their admonitions to heart.

The media do not seem to be at pains to point out that the Pill and other precautions have not stopped the increase of the birthrate outside marriage. According to the figures given by the National Council for One Parent Families the highest percentage of illegitimate births was in 1945 — the year the war ended — when it was 9.3 per cent. In 1947 it had dropped to 5.3 per cent and continued to stay down until 1962 when it rose to 6.6 per cent. The figure for 1976 was 9.1 per cent. Of this figure two-thirds were born to girls under twenty-five; 20,000 of them to parents both of whom were born in Britain, and the birthplace of 24,000 of the fathers was not stated. The number of abortions performed on single women in that year was 50,481.

When we first started the Bureau very few women with illegitimate children came to see us. We always did our best to take them on if we could, but it was more difficult to find men to meet them than it is now and we could accept only a very few. We never took them on if they had just had the baby as we felt that they would be looking more for a father for the child than a husband for themselves, and might well fall out of the frying pan into the fire. The one or two that we did manage to help tended to marry men who had either been illegitimate themselves or else had been brought up by one parent.

Several times we had frightened little girls coming to see us saying that they must get married at once. I remember one poor little thing, who looked about six-months pregnant, telling me that she had not told her parents, who lived in the north, and had not even dared go to see them. Another heartbreaking case was the girl who came to us for an immediate father because, unless we could find her one, she would have to sign adoption papers for her child as she could not afford to keep it. She said, I remember, 'I have so little time to make up my mind.' We always tried to give good advice as to who could help, but there was little assistance available then, and they were in a far worse predicament because of public opinion.

The problem as I have said started to get worse in the

sixties and one bureau tried to make capital out of the tragic situation. It was the Kathleen Kent Bureau in Lincolnshire, run by a woman called Stella Groschel. I read some of her advertisements and wrote to two hundred newspaper editors asking them to ban them. On 16 March 1966 the *Daily Mail* printed a feature on her bureau. 'Miss Jenner's letter', it ran, 'says that the advertisements seem to imply that the Bureau is in some sense a Welfare Organisation.' Its reporter who investigated the bureau went on to say, 'This impression is strengthened by advertisements for husbands for unmarried mothers under the heading Welfare Section. We consider this to be contrary to all principles on which a reputable marriage bureau should be founded.'

In the same article Mrs Groschel was reported to have said, 'There is a definite need for this kind of Welfare Service for unmarried mothers and widows with children in the Welfare State. By helping unmarried mothers in finding nice husbands we do take them off the state. They could cost you or me hundreds of pounds through our life times. We do something really definite for these people.'

The next day, 17 March, the *Daily Mail* carried the story again and went further, reporting that a mentally retarded man of twenty-eight was put in touch with an unmarried girl who was three-months pregnant when he answered an advertisement from the Kathleen Kent Introduction Bureau. Part of Mrs Groschel's evasive and unsatisfactory answer to this was: 'We have an executive and farming section as well as this unmarried mother angle. There is no other way of doing it.'

I was quoted as saying that advertisements for unmarried mothers are dangerous because they attract girls who are vulnerable. Mrs Bramhall, then Secretary of the National Council for the Unmarried Mother and Her Child (now the National Council for One Parent Families, of which she is a director) said, 'Potentially it is very dangerous indeed for pregnant girls to go to marriage bureaux. Pregnant girls feel isolated. They need time to face up to their problems.'

The unmarried mothers who come to see us now are different; they are usually treated with much more understanding by their families, and can find out how to get help if they are not. The first time I realised how much opinion all over the country had changed was when a very beautiful girl, who had had an illegitimate child a few years before, came to see me. She told me that while she was pregnant she had stayed with her parents in a small suburb of a large provincial town where her family had lived for generations. She had expected to be ostracised and even insulted, but had met with nothing but kindness. Even the people whom she had though stuffy and old fashioned knitted things for the baby and cooed over it in its pram.

Some time ago we had a question added to the form asking men whether they would meet unmarried mothers. Of a hundred I picked out at random thirty-two gave an unequivocal 'yes'. Ten said that they possibly would, and two that they would if they knew all the circumstances. One would take on an illegitimate child only if it was very young, and a man of fifty-seven said that he would do so only if it was over twenty. Another man of seventy said that he could not while his mother was alive, and four said that they would if the mother had only one child; another was prepared to, but thought that it might make married life more difficult.

Of the forty-eight who said 'no', one was a man of seventy and another a man of sixty-three; one wrote 'preferably not'; twenty-five were under thirty-five and wanted to meet single girls and start a family of their own; eight older men did not want to meet people with any sort of children; one didn't even want children of his own; nine would meet a woman with a child if it could be with its father some of the time; and one simply crossed the question through.

The girls with illegitimate children who come to us are

reticent; they tell us the facts without embellishing them. Often they have had an affair with a married man on the understanding that he would get a divorce from his wife, but he did not do so. One mother who is with us has had two children by the same father. After the first child when he did not part from his wife she did not see him again for a couple of years. Then he came back and she fell again—he is still married, but helps to support her and the children. Phyllida, who comes from a well-to-do middle-class family, has been cut off by them, in almost *East Lynne* fashion, although she has the child to look after. She is on the bread line and, unused to fending for herself, is not good at claiming the extras to which she is entitled. All these girls wanted marriage in the first place, and some said that they had had the baby to make sure that the father would marry them.

It is difficult to know how many of the illegitimate children are born by mistake and how many deliberately. A few women have been to us because they wanted to get married, but not to the father of their child. One was a talented and successful woman who loved the father, but said he had a weak character and would be nothing but a liability as a husband. He had at last, to her relief, stopped pestering her to marry him and married somebody else. He still saw the child whenever he wished. She would now like to meet a man whom she could love and marry.

The other woman was rich, wayward and spoilt—those were her words—she was certainly beautiful, amusing and unconventional. She told me that she wasn't quite sure who the father was because she had been sleeping around at the time. Now that the child was at boarding school and showing every sign of being independent rather than a mother's boy, she wanted a man to marry.

Stories vary about how well single parents can manage and how much help they can get from the state. I think that it is worse for girls like Phyllida who have been used to a high standard of living and few responsibilities — she had always been helped by her family until they rejected her — than for girls who come from low-income homes. Mary was one of these, she had supported herself since she had left school at sixteen. She came to me because she wanted to get married, but a workmate of hers had told her that it was silly to get married. The workmate, Lucy, a girl who had lived in this country for only four years, had left her family in another country and was very independent. She had had a child because she wanted one, but she did not want a husband. She lived in a two-room council flat. Mary had visited her there and said that it was not in a very good district, nor in very good condition, but Lucy was not unhappy as she was hoping to get a three-room flat soon. Mary understood that the baby was looked after free while Lucy worked, that Lucy received allowances on her electricity, and managed to claim other benefits. She was entitled to a sum each week too, but she earned a great deal more by working. She often saw the child's father of whom she was fond, but they had both agreed that they were better off living apart. Lucy had been lucky, and energetic in applying for assistance. Even with assistance many single-parent families from whatever background have a very hard time. Mary wanted a husband, and only when they could afford a proper home, a baby.

In our book *Men and Marriage* Muriel Segal and I pointed out that a father could be deprived of his child if he did not marry the mother. We added that unmarried fathers were a new problem and that the number of them fighting to obtain recognition of paternity had grown. Their problem has increased since 1970 when we wrote the book and the National Council for One Parent Families is trying to help them. At present if the mother refuses the father access to the child he can make an application under the Guardianship of Infants Act, make the child a ward of court and apply for access or custody. But if the mother has the child adopted, which she can do without his consent, although the father has to be informed, he can do nothing.

The Council is also trying to abolish illegitimacy. As it rightly says, 'It is wrong that a person should be treated in an inferior way simply because of an accident of birth.' It is hoping to change the illegitimacy laws so that, amongst other things, the father of the child should be able to have his name inserted on the birth certificate whether the mother consents or not.

As I have said, two-thirds of the illegitimate babies in 1976 were born to girls under twenty-five. Of these girls 1,512 were under sixteen, the youngest being eleven. Girls in the sixteen to nineteen age group gave birth to 18,980 illegitimate babies. Most of these births must have been accidental.

This swinging Permissive Age has not lived up to its light-hearted name. Perhaps after the first wave of freedom we will settle down and want to give it another name, something like the Age of Reconsideration.

4 The Law

*I know no method to secure the repeal
of bad or obnoxious laws so effective as
their stringent execution.*

ULYSSES SIMPSON GRANT

Until the beginning of this century the legal marrying age in
this country was according to Roman Law. The age of
consent was fourteen for males and twelve for females, but
they could not make marriage settlements on each other
until the male was twenty and the female seventeen. Women
were the property of their husbands and had the same legal
status as a lunatic or a child. In 1929 the age of consent was
raised to sixteen for both sexes, and those under twenty-one
had to have the consent of their parent or guardian if they
wanted to marry. Thus in two world wars young men of
eighteen could be conscripted to fight and to be killed, but
they could not marry without permission.

In 1969 the legal marrying age was lowered to eighteen.
This was chiefly because the courts could not keep up with
so many people being made Wards in Chancery: they
married abroad or just lived together. The age of consent
has been kept the same and many people think that it
should be lowered to fourteen. This idea was put forward
officially by the National Council of Civil Liberties, but the
Senate of the Courts, an organisation of judges and
barristers, was against it, although it admitted that sexual
intercourse with girls under sixteen had greatly increased in
recent years.

In the Marriage Bureau we never take on anybody under
the legal age for marrying, and often we cannot take on
some of the very young men who come to us unless they are
in well-established jobs. Girls in that age group usually want

47

to marry somebody a bit older than themselves. The reason these young people come to us is nearly always because they have left home early, sometimes immediately after leaving school.

During the last 120 years the divorce laws have changed more quickly than at any other time since Henry VIII broke with the Church of Rome. Before 1858 it was impossible to get a divorce except by act of parliament, which was expensive and beyond the reach of most people. One man accused of bigamy was told by a judge:

You should have instituted a suit in the Ecclesiastical Court for a divorce. Having got that divorce you should have petitioned the House of Lords and should have appeared by counsel at the bar of their Lordship's House. Then if the Bill was passed, it would go down to the House of Commons; the same evidence would be repeated there; and if the Royal assent had been given after that, you might marry again. The whole proceeding would not have cost you more than a thousand pounds.

To which the poor man replied, 'Ah, my Lord, I never was worth a thousand pence in all my life.'

From the beginning of 1858 a husband could sue his wife for adultery only through the courts. She was not allowed to appear or to be represented in her defence. If a wife wanted to sue her husband for the same offence she had to prove bigamy, rape, cruelty, or desertion for at least two years as well; and if she won her case he could still keep her money and her children. The Married Woman's Property Act of 1870 allowed a wife to keep her earnings and after another act in 1882 her property, too.

The strong feelings about the wrongness of divorce gradually changed. To begin with, divorced people were ostracised. Many of them went to live abroad if they could afford it; it was less painful than being cut by society at home. By the thirties and forties divorce had become more acceptable, but the law insisted on a guilty party; and it became the gentlemanly thing for the man to be divorced if a couple wanted to end a marriage. Until 1938 this could be arranged if the husband spent one night in an hotel with a professional co-respondent. The chief evidence seemed to be through the maid who brought them their breakfast in bed the next morning. A 'good' solicitor would arrange all this for his client by putting him in touch with the right people and the right hotel. This was stopped on the grounds that the real facts were cloaked by an artificial procedure and divorce again became more complicated. Cruelty, drunkenness, and refusal of conjugal rights were brought in as justifiable grounds, which in many ways made the process still more artificial.

After the last war husbands became less gallant. It was often the wife who wanted to remarry and the husband would have to pay all the expenses and alimony if he allowed himself to be named as the guilty party. Collusion occurred. The wife, to preserve her reputation, would waive the alimony; in fact many sensible arrangements made by husband and wife rather than by the courts would, if discovered, have made it absolutely certain that a divorce would not be granted.

Private detective agencies reaped a rich harvest establishing the facts of the guilty party's misdemeanours. As the evidence of one night was insufficient, the couple had to be followed for longer. One of my clients told me that he took a woman to a cottage lent to him by a friend and had arranged with his wife that they would be followed. It poured with rain and to his amazement the woman whom he had taken with him, a professional co-respondent, said what a pity it was that they could not get a bridge four. They could see the detectives' car 'hidden' round the corner so he went out and asked them if they could play. They could and did so for the rest of the weekend.

Another client who was a friend of mine told me about his divorce. His wife was very attractive and he had for years taken it for granted that she was unfaithful. He was not happy, but she was a good mother and ran their house well so he put up with her infidelities. He worked in the City and one of his friends there who knew the situation thought he looked ill, and suggested that he came to stay with him and his wife for a week in the country. My client accepted as he had known the wife almost as long as he had known the husband and liked them both. He realised it would be an excellent opportunity to get away and think things out. During the week he was there the husband had to stay a night in London. Unbeknown to my client his wife, who wanted to marry someone else, had had him followed. He had never gone away on his own before and she smelt a rat; so the night that the husband was away the detectives who had been watching the house became really active. Having discovered after several nights' observation which was the main bedroom, one of them climbed up an old magnolia tree underneath the bedroom window as soon as the lights went on to see what was going on. The branch that he was sitting on broke and he fell to the ground with a crash and a yell. The wife looked out of the window and yelled for my client to go down and see what was happening while she rang the police. The man had broken his arm and had to explain to the police that he was not a burglar or a peeping tom, but a private detective. My client realised that his wife would get a report about this, but simply telephoned her and said that he was staying on for another week, without mentioning the accident. During that week he had her followed and consequently got a divorce.

Solicitors, too, had a profitable time giving their clients half-hour interviews to initiate them into the ways that mental cruelty could be proved. Losing weight and asking one's doctor for sedatives and sleeping pills were splendid weapons. Backed up by a certificate from the doctor saying how bad his patient's nerves were, due to worry, it was a point made. One of my clients whose solicitor suggested this course of action told me that she had put on weight after she married because she was so bored. She took the solicitor's advice and slimmed, but it made her feel and look marvellous. When she came to see me a few years after the divorce — still looking marvellous — she told me that as she got slimmer she realised how much she had let herself go, and started dressing better as well. It was vanity reawakened, but as she said, it helped her case not at all. Her solicitor was horrified when he saw her looking so well, but luckily she had asked her doctor for many more sleeping pills than she had ever needed, and obtained a divorce on his evidence.

Many people were committing perjury in the divorce courts as the only way to be sure of winning their case. One woman told me how she lost the custody of her child. She said, quite truthfully, that she could afford only a small flat and that her home was not as nice as her husband's. It was also in a town whereas he lived in the country, and for this reason she was prepared to let the child stay with her husband for long intervals. She lost her case.

Another woman who had been the wife of a doctor said that a letter was read out in court from a responsible person saying that the child would like to be a doctor 'like daddy'. The boy was seven when he said this, had always hated the smell of the surgery and was sometimes upset when he saw seriously ill patients. He also fainted when he saw blood. But one can easily imagine that if the child with his father beside him was asked the question by a total stranger his instinct would be to say yes as the shortest and easiest way out of the situation.

By the sixties more and more of our clients would meet divorced people but many would say that they did not want to meet the guilty party. This naturally enough applied even more if the divorce was for cruelty, as nobody could be certain whether it had been a trumped-up case or not.

Happily, on 1 January 1971 the Divorce Reform Act became law and since then the only grounds for divorce in England and Wales is the irretrievable breakdown of the marriage, if the parties concerned have been married (except in a few exceptional cases) for three years. There is no guilty party and, provided there are no children of the marriage and one party notifies the court and the other consents, nobody has to appear in court. If there are children under sixteen the couple have to appear to make sure that the children are properly provided for. Divorce can also be given for adultery if the partner and co-respondent notify the court that they will not defend, and after five years' separation if the partner does not intend to defend.

This law takes the sting out of divorce. And a very sensible clause says that if a couple co-habit for less than six months during the separation time of two years in the hope that it might bring them together again, it does not stop the original petition, or even hold it up.

We do not take on people who are separated but not divorced, the chief reason being that as we are a Marriage Bureau we only take on people who are free to marry. I have known several 'separated' couples make it up with or without co-habiting. Having tasted freedom they felt lonely and, particularly if they had children, missed a complete home life.

Recently one of our clients — tall, dark and very attractive — who had got a divorce through the new laws after a separation of two years, said at the end of the interview, 'By the way — don't introduce me to X., she told me that she was one of your clients and to come to you. My ex-wife is now married to her husband.' It was lucky that the client mentioned this because my interviewer had been thinking that X. would have been suitable.

Women complain that their husbands don't listen to them, and after a day spent doing housework and shopping they want somebody to talk to. If they work they are as tired as their husbands when they get home, but they are the ones who are expected to cook, settle problems about children's clothes and ailments, and, as one of them put it, put in another good day's work.

One ex-wife told me that she had to entertain a number of her husband's business friends and their wives. Some of them became her friends, but in the long run she found them rather boring. Her husband, however, would never admit that this could possibly be so. 'If only he could have joked about it a bit with me,' she said, 'it would have been all right, but he got cross and seemed to think that they were all perfect and I was dreadful, and what is worse, everything he does is business, even playing golf or bridge.'

When this sort of pressure accumulates it leads to grievances, real or imagined, which end in quarrels. Some couples thrive on these, and I have heard them lovingly describe them. The majority of people, however, hate them: accusations that are brought up during quarrels stick and leave scars; they also show up lies and broken promises. Complete indifference is another and often worse consequence. A woman told me that after a few years of marriage to her husband he ignored her existence. She was an actress and very vivacious. I suppose that after a few years she bored him, but his frigid politeness and lack of interest in anything she said or did drove her to desert him.

People whose parents were divorced sometimes talk about the effect that it had on them as children. Some had hoped that it wouldn't be found out when they were at school. One of my greatest friends at school had a beautiful mother whose surname was different from her own. She never told me anything about her mother and I never dared ask her; I merely worked out from the facts I knew that she was not a widow who had remarried — she must have been divorced.

By the late fifties and sixties so many children seemed to have two sets of parents that nobody was particularly concerned. Some of them found it an advantage because they get the best out of both their parents and the variety of more than one home.

A number of people who now come to us have had common-law marriages. In our experience so far these marriages have not lasted very long. But sometimes the relationship follows the pattern of a real marriage. I read in the paper recently of a man with a common-law wife by whom he had had ten children. Until the thirteenth century, when the Church stepped in and tried to stop them, these marriages were common in Britain and were recognised as a private contract between two individuals reinforced by the community sense of what was right. In spite of the Church, the habit of private contract between two individuals continued in country districts and was accepted as a form of marriage, particularly in Scotland. There, if both parties signed the family bible in front of witnesses it was recognised as marriage. During the war when marriage and family allowances were introduced there was a rush to the registry office in many districts by respectably 'married' couples.

Now there seems to be no definite ruling; a so-called and usually self-called common-law husband and wife are under the same law as two people just living together, and I have asked why the common-law pair have been so insistent on bringing in the word marriage. The answer has almost invariably been: 'We made promises to each other; we did not think we needed a ceremony and all the fuss.'

People who have simply been living together sometimes say that they were sad when the affair broke up; others can be quite funny about it. One eligible and dishy bachelor said he'd had several narrow escapes. He would have an affair with a girl who would gradually start moving in. The first one who did this brought her make-up and moved in more and more clothes; then he found a dressing table in his bedroom one day, and frilly pillows and exotic sheets followed. Next he came back from work and found her painting the kitchen. Then he really saw the red light, and told her she would have to go. He realised that she was trying to trap him by putting so much work into the flat that if he tried to turn her out she would want to claim compensation for all she had done. Since then, he said, one suitcase worth was all he had allowed. Anyhow, he had had enough of that way of life and now wanted a wife.

Sex discrimination is no longer an issue in many aspects of marital affairs; in fact some people, even some women, think that the law has gone too far in favour of women. I felt this with a client of mine. He had a large property which he farmed, and was a rich man. When he and his wife divorced he had to give her his flat in London and sell off valuable land to give her the money that was awarded to her. Looking desperate he said to me, 'I can't make another mistake, if I did I would have to sell more land and would not have a livelihood.'

The Inland Revenue, however, correct the balance in their chauvinist way: if husbands' and wives' incomes are separately assessed, the man receives the major allowances. He used also to receive the allowances for a child if he married a woman who already had one. This law was changed in 1978 provided the couple married, but if they only live together the woman loses her child benefits. Perhaps if women complain enough they will get equal treatment in this too.

The greatest unfairness in the law is nothing to do with sex, it is to do with money, and is to the disadvantage of anybody in the middle-income group. A woman who later became a client told me how she and her ex-husband had had a legal battle in court. She had won her appeal, and he had then won his appeal against that decision. She was given leave to appeal to the House of Lords, but it meant putting down a large sum of money which she simply did not have. If she had had less money she might possibly have been granted legal aid. This injustice goes right through the legal system—whatever the case—and presumably a great fuss will have to be made before it is remedied.

5 Love

He first deceased—she for a little tryd
To live without him liked it no and dyd.

SIR HENRY WOOTTON

Ever since those first days in 1939 I have been asked by people interested in the Marriage Bureau if my clients fall in love. The answer is that they do, sometimes to their surprise. A man of thirty-five wrote:

Will you please call off any further introductions and erase my name from your books? I am caught, hook, line and sinker—and further letters will now be rather embarrassing. Later when I have had time to 'come round' I will write you again in detail. Let me however say that staid and set as I was in my bachelor existence I have never in my wildest dreams imagined that there existed a girl in England with the power to so completely change my outlook and make me fall so deeply in love. Yet it is so and I am very happy.

Love between men and women is a complicated emotion, and married love is still more difficult. In the sixteenth century it was looked upon as a disease that needed treatment, often administered harshly, to hasten the cure. Marriage was for the good of the family and not the end product of love. Two centuries later *The Lady's Magazine* still felt the same way: 'Matrimony was not for man and wife to be always taken up with each other, but jointly to discharge the duties of civil society, to govern their families and educate their children with discretion.'

It was at this period that romantic novelists began to

emerge in Britain. Nice girls did not read Harriet Wilson, *Fanny Hill* or French novels. They read Fanny Burney's *Evelina* and Jane Austen's novels about pure young women who ended in marrying above their station. These novelists were followed by the Brontë sisters who, except for Emily in *Wuthering Heights*, wrote about the same thing. Queen Victoria loved her husband and said so, and her prime minister, Disraeli, also wrote romantic novels. Romance was in the air and marrying for love rather than for family crept in. The girls were, however, well chaperoned.

Elinor Glyn broke the tradition of the woman getting her man only in wedlock, and introduced the idea of the woman taking the initiative. In *Three Weeks* the seductress of the well-brought up young Englishman, Paul, was an Imperial Highness whose husband was a brute. The end product of their illicit love was a fair-haired boy who succeeded to the Imperial throne. The book sold nearly two million copies throughout the English-speaking world. An enormous number for 1907.

During this century the tradition of the virtuous girl getting her man has been carried on by such novelists as Berta Ruck, Ursula Bloom and Barbara Cartland, and also by those who write short stories for women's magazines. Their heroines remain pure and *intacta* until they get to the altar, after which they live happily ever after. Younger novelists are at present much more concerned with reality and as often as not deal with the problems of those who do not live happily ever after.

The sex symbols of the early cinema behaved circumspectly—at any rate on the screen. Rudolph Valentino and later Clark Gable, even if they started the film as a lecherous sheikh, as in the case of Valentino, or as a dashing cad, in the case of Clark Gable, were eventually tamed and they made an honest woman of the heroine.

The pop groups are different from the stars of the cinema who rarely appear in England in public. They are young boys who are seen in the flesh. Many of them are British and come from the same sort of backgrounds as their fans. They often marry quite ordinary-sounding and looking British girls. They are attainable, and their fan clubs are made up mainly of girls influenced by this. Many of these girls grow out of their hero-worshipping phase, and even laugh about it when they are older; but with some the hysteria gives them a real sexual thrill and they look around for boys who will satisfy it, romantically or in fact. When I was writing a weekly column for a group of provincial newspapers I used to get letters from teenagers saying that they were in love with boys who looked like one of their favourite stars. One girl aged thirteen wrote that a boy who was the image of her favourite pop star lived in the same road as she did and they often waited at the bus stop together. He was about fifteen, blushed when he saw her, but never spoke. Should she speak to him first?

I gave her a decided 'yes'. He sounded young, shy and inexperienced so it was better for her to fix her calf love on him than on somebody more dangerous.

In 1939 girls were no longer heavily chaperoned and many of them were just longing to meet some gorgeous man, look into his eyes, see love in them and live happily ever after. Now girls are more practical. But love at first sight does exist and is all the better for being unexpected. It is marvellous when it happens and it happens at all ages. It may last for ever or end in calamity. I am a great believer in it, but I do not think that it should lead to immediate marriage. For that reason, although I am thrilled when two clients tell me that the love between them started the moment they met, I like to hear that they are not getting married at once, but are meeting each other's families and friends, and getting to know each other really well first. We have in fact had very few engagements broken off by couples who as soon as they meet felt that they would be right for each other. Recently one couple — both in their fifties — fell in love at their first meeting and became engaged a few weeks later. They then quarrelled and broke off the engagement. We waited. Neither of them wanted any more introductions, and then months later, after making up their quarrel, they saw each other again and got married.

The sad fact, though, is that it is possible to keep on falling in love at first sight. Some people make a habit of it and fall out of love again just as quickly. Cynthia, feminine and romantically inclined, was one of those people in love with love. She told us that she had frequently fallen in love at first sight, and that she had come to us so that she would have a suitable choice of people with whom she could fall in love. My interviewer asked her what had happened to all the ex-loved ones, and if she had been engaged to any of them. She said that she had to one or two, but had always broken it off when she came to know them better. She really did want a husband and children and to be a homemaker. My interviewer was just about to tell her that she thought that she was too immature and should wait a bit before she got married when Cynthia said that her parents had got married through us. I looked them up and then remembered the mother. She had broken off two engagements to our clients, but her eventual marriage seemed to have lasted. My interviewer had a brilliant idea. She told Cynthia that if she fell in love at first sight with one of our clients she was to tell us and we would send her another introduction whom she must meet, and we would ask the man to meet somebody else too. This had a remarkable effect. Several men said how much they had liked her, but Cynthia didn't seem to respond. Then a man who had been her fourth introduction wrote and told us that he had fallen in love with her and she had turned him down. He didn't want any more introductions for the moment. He could think of nobody but her. He had written to her often, but she wrote back non-committal notes.

At least she answered, I thought. We wrote and asked her

to come in for another interview, and asked her if she liked the man at all. 'Oh, yes, very much,' replied Cynthia, 'but he put me off because he told me he had fallen in love with me the first moment he saw me. He must be like I used to be.'

He came in for a second interview, too, and assured us that he had never fallen in love like that before. It ended happily in marriage and we have a Christmas card from them every year.

Physical attraction is one of the chief causes of love at first sight: it can be sheer good looks, the way a person smiles, the way they move their hands, their features, their hair, the texture of their skin, or their smell. It can also be a mental or spiritual attraction, the way they put forward their ideas, their humour, or their sophistication.

We ask our clients to describe the physical type that they find attractive. Some of the men will have very definite ideas. They specify the exact height, weight, colouring and type, often giving as an example some well-known beauty. The women, unless very young, are not so insistent on actual looks, but they nearly always ask to meet a man taller than themselves, and may say that they do or do not like bald or fat men. A widow who was very tall told me that her husband had been much shorter than she was. They had been happy together, but she felt that she had loved him in spite of his lack of height. Now she would prefer to meet taller men.

Stephanie, who was twenty-one and six foot tall said that she did not mind meeting somebody a bit shorter. She got engaged to a man of five foot ten and then wrote, 'I am embarrassed when we go out because I am so much taller than he is although I wear low heels. I want him to wear shoes with lifts in them, but he says that I have to accept him as he is. I have heard people making remarks about us when we pass them, but I cannot make John change his mind.'

I wrote back and told her that I thought he was right, if

he didn't worry why should she? I suggested that she ought to consider whether she was really in love with him or not. She decided that she wasn't, and eventually married a man of six foot three.

We are handicapped by these specifications. Very often tall women are attracted by shorter men, and plenty of short men seemed to love both large women and large cars. On paper, though, they will not admit this. In what I call outside life, meaning not through the Marriage Bureau, the most unlikely people will meet and fall in love with someone quite different from the sort of person we have been asked to find for them. Two people will meet and discover an affinity which they would never have thought possible.

A woman wrote, 'You know I asked you to find me a tall fair-skinned Englishman under forty. Well I'm marrying a man of South American origin who's about five foot four. He has large melting dark brown eyes and is over fifty.' To soften the blow she added, 'He's very anglicised now, he's lived here for years.'

A man rang up and said, 'I'm marrying somebody completely different from the sort of girl I described to you.' I congratulated him and hoped that he would be happy. I took out his form and looked at it. He had written on it that he didn't much mind about religion, colouring, or height — he was tall himself — nor was he very interested in education and he did not want an intellectual sort of wife. The things that he was most insistent about were that the girl should be under thirty, single and prepared to have children, and a non-smoker. Also, preferably, he wanted somebody who did not mind him playing cricket in the summer and watching football in the winter. I imagined him marrying a chain-smoking woman well over the age of child bearing who stayed indoors reading poetry all day and dragged him off to concerts at night.

People, too, will change their types. One man came into the office and said to me as I went in to interview him,

'Good Heavens! You're the image of my first wife.' He then proceeded to ask for my opposite in looks.

After meeting a few people who accord as nearly as possible with the type that they asked for some of our clients change their minds and come back for a re-interview. Allen who had asked to meet intelligent girls said, 'I don't want to meet an intellectual ball of fire after all. Somebody acquainted with the three R's, with plenty of common sense and curves in the right places will do.'

Another man who had insisted he must meet blondes wrote, 'I asked for a blonde, but am not as certain that even real ones turn me on. Find me a slim and vivacious girl. She'll always change the colour of her hair if she wants to anyhow.'

Susan had said most particularly on her form that she disliked men with beards. I sent her a very good-looking and clean-shaven man whom I had interviewed a few months before. She wrote me a furious letter. Since I had seen him he had grown a beard. She met other people but didn't want to marry any of them. The man then decided he didn't much like his beard and shaved it off. As he had liked her better than anybody else he'd met he wrote to her, told her that he was now clean shaven and suggested another meeting. I had a letter from her on her honeymoon in which she said, 'I am very glad he shaved off his beard, it would have been terrible if he hadn't and we had never met again. If he grows one again I shall complain, but I suppose I will have to put up with it. At the moment he says he wouldn't dream of doing such a thing.'

Mental love, Shakespeare's 'marriage of true minds', can make a marriage stronger. If two people genuinely love the arts, sport, or travelling, for example, they will always have that in common. If one of them knows nothing about the other's special interest but would like to learn that can be a great boon. We ask our clients about their leisure interests and hobbies. But if a man says he is fond of golf and sport it is often worth probing more deeply. The British are usually modest. Some do just play golf, but we have had a client who bashfully admitted when questioned further that his handicap was scratch. Many people say that they are fond of music. We ask them what sort? Classical, jazz, trad, or pop? We also ask them if they play a musical instrument, and if they say they like classical music we ask them what composers they like best, and if they go to concerts or listen on tapes or records. When I asked one girl if she went to concerts she replied, 'Yes, often.' She then mentioned that her half-brother was a well-known classical pianist. Another of our clients sings in a famous choir and another is a composer who is becoming well known. In contrast, one client we had was tone deaf and said that he did not want to meet anybody who was fond of music, it irritated him to hear it.

A keen yachtsman who was asked if he would like his wife to be one too said, in a voice weary with experience, 'Only if she's a good sailor. There's nothing worse than having a sea-sick woman on board.'

Other men and women will fall in love with somebody with a good brain. The cleverer the person the fewer peers they have, and in marriage they may settle for somebody who is not as intelligent as they are but whom they think will make a good marriage partner. In this I think that there is —consciously or unconsciously—sexual discrimination. Men are much less likely to love a woman for her brains, particularly if she is more intelligent than they are and it is their subject. Women are more prepared to be pupils, and will even pretend ignorance to flatter a man. This attitude is dying out, but we still come across it occasionally.

On our forms we ask our clients to fill in details of their education. A man who has gained the highest degrees himself will often say that he would like to meet a woman who is well educated, but he does not insist that she has reached an equally high standard. A woman will invariably ask to meet somebody whose education is as good as hers or better. One man at the top of his profession said he would like to meet a woman similarly placed but only if she was in a different profession from his.

An actor wanted to meet somebody connected with the stage, but he wanted to be the main wage earner and said that it would be better if the girl was not too ambitious. He had seen so many stage marriages crack up because the husband and wife had been apart so much. In other words he wanted his wife to fit in with his plans — if she was more famous than he was, he would not like sacrificing any work that he might get to fit in with hers. He was very handsome and charming, and definitely chauvinist, but we found the perfect person for him. She had talent and had been to RADA, but she lacked the drive and dedication to get very far in the theatrical world. She loved the company of actors, and had played small parts and even been an assistant stage manager at one time simply to be with them, if only on the fringe. She was delighted at the thought of basking in his reflected glory, which was just what he wanted.

Intellectuals often wish to marry their like, but someone preferably in another sphere. A successful author told us that he would like to marry somebody creative, but not a novelist; a musician, a painter or a journalist perhaps. He said, quite frankly, that he thought he would be jealous of a writer.

An older writer of erudite books which only had small sales was a widower. His late wife had written serials, under various names, for provincial newspapers and magazines and had made much more money than he had. They both called it 'her trash', but she wrote it easily and it meant that he had enough money to work at leisure. They had had no children and she had left him comfortably off. Their relationship had been based on intellectual attraction and they had been very happy. Now he wanted to marry a woman who would be a loving companion. He stipulated that she must like the country as he hated towns.

We suggested that he should have a wife who had some special interests, and he agreed. This nearly upset everything. We introduced him to Margaret. She was placid and pretty and quite comfortably off and her hobby was growing roses. They agreed that they would like to marry, but there were problems as he did not want to leave his house, and she did not want to leave her garden. Eventually he gave way as it was more sensible for him to move his books than for her to move her roses.

Mental love is mixed up with spiritual love. In the best spiritual match a couple believe in the same moral values and creeds or, if they do not entirely agree, each holds to his or her own genuine beliefs and allows the same freedom to the other.

A number of clergymen come to us for wives, largely because the spinsters and widows of their parish are apt to look too favourably upon them. As one clergyman said to me, 'I find one or two of my parishioners very attractive, but dare not pursue any special friendship with any of these ladies. If I did so and discovered that one of us did not love the other enough to marry, it would become the talk of the parish and it could only happen once. If it happened more often I would get a bad reputation.'

The same sort of love is sometimes felt towards doctors, and doctors who are setting up in their own practice often feel safer when they are married, especially in country districts where people are more interested in their private lives than they are in the comparative anonymity of a large town.

Together with these three main forces, physical, mental and spiritual, real affection plays an important part in a happy marriage and can outlast the other three initial attractions. Affection is kind, less demanding than love, and therefore more forgiving. It can be a protective instinct and every human being needs to feel protective to someone or something. Affection rarely turns to hatred. Love is much more likely to.

When I had my office in Paris I was interested to see how my French clients used to emphasise affection rather than love. In married matters they are much more practical than the English.

A woman in her forties whose husband had been killed in a car smash came to see me a year after his death and told me how her marriage had been kept together by affection and how much she missed him. She was beautiful and soignée. 'We were married when we were both in our twenties,' she said. 'We had two children, but for the last ten years of our marriage we never had sex together. I had boy friends and he had girl friends but we did not have many quarrels. Not long before he died we wondered whether we should split up or not, but decided against it. He said that he'd fallen physically for several girls, but had never felt the affection for them that he felt for me, and I felt the same way. I know we would have had a very happy old age together. We knew we would never be lonely.' I have been told by many married people that although they had stayed together for years they had been lonely, so I appreciated her last remark.

A man whose wife had run off with somebody else said: 'I was not unduly upset. She was marvellous in bed, and decorative out of it, but she was terribly spoilt and a fool; I had no real affection for her, only physical attraction.' He then went on to say that he wanted to meet another beautiful woman, but he wasn't specific about her education or her interests. We told him that he was asking for trouble again and he admitted that he probably was. We worried about him a lot, but we had time to send him only one introduction before he rang us up to say that he had met somebody at a party. He would let us know what happened. We haven't heard from him since, but I happen to know that he has not remarried. Maybe he has learnt some caution.

When affection is protective, a woman may feel that a

man needs looking after and enjoy seeing to his comforts; or a man may like to explain to his wife exactly where the Gulf Stream flows or how the clutch of a car works. He may sometimes yearn for the palmy days of bachelorhood when he could leave his belongings wherever he wanted, and she may not listen to the whole of his educational explanations, but in the long run they will work out well together. She will put on an attentive look and let him hold forth, and he will really be pleased that his home is neat and well cared for.

A few years ago we had a very touching example of unselfish love and attraction between a couple. Mr Willis came to see us after his wife had died of cancer. She had been ill for four years. Just before she died she told him that after she had gone, but not before, he was to look in a certain drawer in her writing desk. When he did so he found a copy of *Woman's Journal* dated two years before, open at a page on which they had printed our advertisement. This she had drawn a line around. He came to see us eighteen months later and I am glad to say he is now happily married.

Recently, however, a frightening thing happened. An elderly man whose wife had died two days before and was not yet buried wanted to join the Bureau. He said that he had adored his wife and wanted to meet her exact replica. He insisted on making out a cheque for us. After half an hour of trying to persuade him that he should wait for a little while, my interviewer, realising he was in a state of shock, took the cheque. We then wrote to him a few days later and told him that we would not cash it, but would hold it and perhaps he would come and see us again in a few months' time. We would be here, we said, and would help him when we could.

I do not look upon love as a disease, as they did three hundred years ago, but it can have its maladies: particularly jealousy, possessiveness and selfishness. Most people have suffered from one or more of these feelings at some time as they are natural human reactions, and can start from an early age. But as a man or a woman grows up they have to learn to adjust to society and if these failings are deep seated they can lead to the destruction of the very people they love most.

We ask our clients to assess their own personalities as well as those of the sort of person whom they would like to meet. Very few of them admit to being jealous. They sometimes admit to being possessive.

A university professor in his fifties, quiet, softly spoken, and looking older than his age, told me about his wife and why they eventually parted. 'If I spoke to another woman at a party she was at my side at once bristling, and sometimes she was rude. She suspected me of being attracted by and making passes at the girls who came to my lectures, although they were all about thirty years younger than I was; and she was even jealous of the time that I spent on my stamp collection.' He asked us for a woman about his own age, placid and good humoured. Anything for a quiet life I felt.

A woman who came to see us said: 'My late husband was very jealous. He would not even let me watch television when I was on my own as he said that I only wanted to look at other men. He would feel the television to see if it was warm when he came into the room to make sure that I had not been watching on the sly. Sometimes he locked my clothes up in a shed when he went to work so that I could not go out. It got so bad that I asked my doctor about it, who said that he should see a psychiatrist. Unfortunately he died of pneumonia and I missed him terribly. I really loved him and he had no cause for his suspicions.'

Felicity, when she came to see us, lived up to her name and was happy and extroverted. She got engaged to David but after a few months came to see us. She was in great distress and had lost all her ebullience, and her looks had changed for the worse. First, David had said that she must get rid of her little dog. She was unhappy about this but his reasoning was sensible: they were going to live in a flat in a town, and the dog had been used to a house with a garden. He said that it would be in kinder to leave it with her parents. Now he was objecting to her seeing her girl friends. He had also taken great exception to her favourite boy cousin. She admitted that in this case, as she had always looked upon her cousin as a brother and they shared lots of jokes in common, she understood his feelings. As David had got the flat she felt that she had to go through with the marriage.

I asked her what her parents thought about it and she told me that they liked him because he seemed reliable, but they were not altogether happy about the match and had told her to come and see me.

I advised her to break off the engagement at once, whatever the consequences. They would be unpleasant, but shorter than the life sentence to which she was committing herself.

Possessiveness can be charming. The fact that somebody is interested enough in you to want to know what you are doing and thinking can be flattering. But at its worst it can be repressive, especially when one partner is forced to give up an interest because the other will not share it and is not able or prepared to try. The saddest sentence to hear from anyone is: 'I used to go to concerts, play tennis [or some such thing] before I was married.'

Love brings an increase in both jealousy and possessiveness, so they are easy to spot before marriage. Selfishness is rather different: people who have scarcely thought of anybody but themselves before will suddenly change and start thinking of their loved one. This *may* last for ever, but after marriage they may well have a relapse.

I can remember only one man who admitted to being selfish. He said he liked to get his own way in everything and that was how he had become a tycoon. He was prepared to be a good husband and generous to any girl he married, but she must respect his wishes. She was to run his home smoothly and be a good hostess, and if they had children she would have to see that they were properly cared for and brought up—they would of course go to the best schools. We found him a girl who wanted that sort of life. Her late husband, also a rich man, had died a few years before, just after they were married. I see pictures of them occasionally in the glossies: they seem to be wearing well and look happy.

A friend of mine who married through me told me her husband-to-be had suggested a honeymoon in an exotic place but, a non-golfer herself, she had been a bit surprised when she saw he had his golf clubs amongst their luggage. It was true she had sometimes watched him play when they were engaged. She said nothing, however, and when a few days after they arrived he fixed up a game of golf, she walked round with them. The course was crowded so that it was very slow and she found it boring, so the next time he went off she stayed at the hotel and sunbathed. 'Luckily,' she said, 'when he came back I was having a drink and talking animatedly to a good-looking and obvious "wolf".' He left soon after her husband arrived saying, 'See you tomorrow, I hope.' There was no more golf on the honeymoon. The symptoms were still there but she always counteracted them. She didn't mind him playing golf, in fact she took it up herself. After they had a child she agreed with him that he must have relaxation at weekends, but insisted that she must have relaxation too, and found an au pair girl so that she was not so tied to the house. I asked her if he was ever cross about her retaliations. 'Oh, no,' she said. 'Just surprised. In his family the men always came first and the women fitted in with their plans, I've just re-educated him.'

In other families a girl can be brought up to believe that she should have things her own way, and marriage may be a revelation if her husband does not agree and insists on having his own way, too.

Janet came from such a family. Ten years younger than her brother, she had been spoilt by both him and their parents. She was exquisitely pretty—auburn hair, large emerald-green eyes, good figure and small bones. When she remembered to look languid she could manage a fragile appeal, but as soon as she forgot one could see that she was tough. She had been a child model, and now because she was so petite modelled teenage clothes; she also modelled hats. My interviewer said, after Janet had left the office, 'What a little Madam.'

The boys who went out with her fell for her at first, but then dropped her. One was more persistent and we thought that they might become engaged, but he dropped her too. He told us that the last straw had been when she had asked him to take her to a six o'clock film in the West End. It had to be early because she was modelling hats the next day and did not want a late night. She lived in Hampstead and because it was raining expected him to leave his office in the City early and fetch her. He said he couldn't manage this, and she slammed the receiver down on him. This he said had been the pattern of her behaviour before, but she had kept better control of herself up to that time.

In the past marriage was easier than it is now. Love did not come into it, and there was no choice about whether a couple should part or not. They stayed together whether they liked it or not until death. Long-lived men and women sometimes had several spouses during their lifetime.

Now it is considered immoral to marry without love, and as divorce is so easy love is all important. Not long ago I heard a story about a man and his wife whose golden wedding day was approaching. A friend of theirs said that she would like to give a party for them. 'I should hate that,' said the wife, 'I'd have to make a speech and wouldn't know what to say. I loathed every minute of my honeymoon and of my married life.' To which her husband replied, 'We could just have a two-minutes' silence.' It was a clever, but bitter reply, and gives a terrible picture of what married life can be like without love.

In all the happiest marriages I have known couples have managed to mix the ingredients of physical, mental and spiritual attraction with affection. In most cases, they have added to the richness of each other's lives and although cherishing each other, neither had made the other a prisoner of their love.

A couple wrote to us after they had celebrated thirty years of marriage with their Pearl Wedding. 'Like everybody else,' the letter said, 'we have had to learn to understand each other and make allowances for each other's failings. I thought that you would like to know that we have managed it and are as happy now as we ever have been—more so in fact.'

6 Companionship

*A crowd is not company, and faces are
not a galaxy of pictures, and talk but a
tinkling cymbal, where there is no love.*

FRANCIS BACON

Early this century Elinor Glyn advised a girl to marry the life
she liked rather than the man she liked, because after a
while the man ceased to matter. Not very flattering to
masculine vanity perhaps, but it could be applied the other
way round and I think that she had a point.

Many couples keep on good terms because they are used
to the same life style. 'County' people often come to our
London office rather than to their local representatives
because they say that they know all the people of their own
kind in their part of the world.

Sir X. was one of these. A widower, he had a large and
lovely house and wanted to meet a woman from his own
background who would be prepared to run it for him. He
was in his sixties, tall, well built, healthy looking, and
conventionally dressed—a rare sight nowadays—gloves,
rolled umbrella, but no hat, the only concession to modern
living. He said that his parents had employed eighteen
indoor servants. Now he had what he called 'rushers in' who
were meant to keep the place clean, and a firm of cleaners
who did it thoroughly twice a year—taking down curtains
and dusting mouldings and friezes. He had modernised the
house as much as he could. The old kitchens were not used
and the old butler's pantry was a kitchen with modern
equipment, the laundry had been modernised too, but he
couldn't get people to work in it. The good linen that had
been so well treated was being ruined by the bleaches that

the local laundry used. He still had a certain amount of land and a syndicate shoot, which he made pay. 'I have to,' he said, 'otherwise I couldn't afford it. Anybody I marry would find it a tough job. It would have to be a woman I loved, too. It's probably impossible,' he added wistfully.

We did have a number of widows with beautiful houses on the books, but they wanted to stay in them. In desperation we tried a very attractive woman who had been a domestic-science teacher. She had been brought up in a large house which her parents had tried to run as a hotel, and when that failed they had sold it. She took one look at Sir X.'s house, liked Sir X., but said that even if he had been Paul Newman she would not have taken it on.

Then Lucy came along to see us in London. The interviewer who saw her was delighted. 'Just the right sort of person for Sir X.,' she said. She went on to explain how the interview had gone. On the form, in answer to the question asking her father's profession, Lucy had written 'Landowner'. Then with a hint of tears in her eyes, she said that she had been an only child and had inherited the property and house, but had had to sell it because of death duties. She added that she might have been able to sell enough land to pay the duties and keep the house which she had loved, but it was pointless. Her son didn't want it, and as if to make this clear he had gone to live in America and become an American citizen. She loved Sir X.'s house at first sight and Sir X. too. As far as I know they have been living happily ever after.

A self-made millionaire held quite opposite views about property. I had interviewed him myself in a large town in the North before I had outside representatives. He had said on his form that he was a manufacturer and that his income varied. I liked him at once. He was expensively but conservatively dressed. He carried a good leather briefcase. His watch was gold and solid looking, not a prestige name one. He wore no signet ring. His voice was quiet with a pleasant North-Country accent. First he showed me snapshots of his house and garden. The garden looked neat and well cared for, and the house was modern. It had four bedrooms, two bathrooms, a drawing room, dining room, TV room, and a kitchen which, he said, was well fitted up. His sister was housekeeping for him at the moment but she agreed with him that it was time he got married, and she wanted to live in a flat of her own in the town. He showed me a few shots of the interior of the house which looked comfortable, but very ordinary. He was forty-eight and said that he had been too busy building up his business to think of marrying before. He then shyly asked if I would like to see a picture of his factory. Out of his briefcase he produced a glossy folder which he opened out like a concertina. It showed an enormous modern factory with his name on the front.

He wanted, he said, to meet a homely sort of woman, preferably a widow in her forties. If she had children he would prefer that they had left home. She must like living quietly and simply. When he got home he liked to relax and forget his business; he never brought work back with him. His recreations were walking, wild flowers and astronomy and he liked going on holidays where he could enjoy the first two of these. Near Annecy in the Haute-Savoie was one of his favourite places.

The enormous factory had completely thrown me. I had been happily thinking in terms of several nice ordinary widows, but now I wondered if they would stay ordinary with all this money about. He seemed sensible enough, but even the hardest-headed businessman can be fooled if he falls in love. I told him that he should meet people from London and the South, and said I would not mention his factory but would put his income down as comfortable. He agreed, but said that if possible he would prefer somebody who came from the North.

Meeting people from London worked quite well. There

were several people he quite liked, then he fell for one of our most pleasant clients. A gentle creature brought up in the Border Country she had had a tragic life — her husband and two children had been killed in a car accident several years before. Left with enough money to live modestly she had devoted her time to working with handicapped children, and wanted to continue to do so if she remarried. She reciprocated his feelings, but when she found out about the money she became alarmed. However he told her that she would not have to wear smart clothes and entertain, and the ordinariness of his house reassured her. Having seen her flat he thought that her taste in furniture was better than his and that she could change anything she wanted. After they were married they often came in to see us when they were in London. He took more time off from work than he had before and they went abroad frequently. She shared his fondness for walking and soon became interested in wild flowers. At home she still helped handicapped children and he was generous in his donations.

Married people are not always lucky enough to be able to afford the way of life that they would like. One girl when asked what sort of house she would like to live in said, 'I'd really like to be a Lady of the Manor, but don't expect to be.' Many couples struggle on through shortage of money, ill health or other hardships. Some relationships will be cemented by shared hard times, others will be divided by them.

Everything had gone wrong in the beginning for one of my young couples who on their tenth wedding anniversary were celebrating in London and came and told me all about it. A few months after they were married he was made redundant and she became pregnant. At first he was too terrified to tell her about the loss of his job because he thought that the shock might bring on a miscarriage. They had a mortgage on the house and had bought things on hire purchase so already had several heavy commitments. When he finally broke the news he found he had underestimated his wife. She reacted energetically and sensibly. First she insisted that it was essential not to keep the crisis a secret from their friends. This was chiefly because she was going to try to borrow clothes and everything else that she wanted for the baby. She would also ask for space in other people's deep freezes so that theirs could be sent back, together with the washing machine, tumble drier and dish washer. She also insisted that he needed to look well turned-out, not down-at-heel, when he was job hunting, so any money for clothes should be spent on his. She was going to look pretty peculiar anyhow as time went on, so she only needed the minimum. He eventually found a good job and they never looked back.

Some people cannot take the hard times and will give up and leave. On the other hand, some will part because they have had too much good luck and have become too prosperous. One of the two cannot keep up with the new style of life and finds it too much of a strain.

Harriet told me that she had been having an affair with a very rich man. He was self-made and married and she explained how the affair ended. He said he would leave his wife and marry her, but kept making excuses not to do so: once it was because his daughter was coming out that year; then he said that his wife had had to have an operation; and after that he said that she made hysterical scenes whenever he mentioned a divorce, and had several times talked of committing suicide. Harriet became suspicious and went round to see his wife. She was calm, good looking, and kind. She said that she did not think that her husband would ever leave her. He liked his home comforts which she saw to, and they were perfectly happy together. She just did not like night life and living it up—she thought that she was too old for it—but her husband did. Tactfully she said that there had been other girl friends, and advised Harriet to launch out a bit and make a social life without him.

Today it is not always the man who makes the money, or

becomes famous. Quite a number of men are known only as the husbands of a successful woman. Sometimes the change of circumstances is unexpected. Eileen told me that she had toed the line and tried to be the perfect wife for several years. She was then left some money by her father. Her husband busily set about telling her how she should use it to their best advantage. To his amazement she had other ideas. She was a very good needlewoman and she started a home industry, making hand-sewn table linen and other household things. Her business grew and soon she bought a sports car, had business lunches which seemed to spread to dinners, and finally they parted.

The attraction of opposites is common. Blondes prefer brunettes, strong people may be attracted to fragile ones; it is nature's way of keeping a balance. Similarly, people of different character can be drawn to one another. A shy man or woman may need somebody gregarious to get them going socially. A successful man may be happier with a woman with whom he can relax mentally and physically and who gives him a home life which is completely different from his business one.

I had a client whom I nicknamed 'Little Nell'. She had soft natural fair hair, a pink and white complexion, and when she filled in her form she had described herself as 'petite'. During the interview she looked at me pathetically and said, 'I've bought myself a dear little house since my husband died. I'm so little though you see. I need a man to help me with cars and income tax and all those difficult things.' She went out with several men who all liked her and said that her house was charming and that she ran it beautifully, but they didn't want to marry her. One said, 'She's too feminine.' Another said, 'She never stops talking and fluttering round.' Then a very brilliant man came to see us. He met one or two women, and said that they were most interesting but that he wanted somebody more domesticated. I introduced him to 'Little Nell' and he was delighted; so was she. He felt protective towards her and her car and income tax problems, and she felt protective towards him and his creature comforts. They were just right for each other and got married. She wrote me a letter saying, 'We are so happy. He even likes "The Archers" as much as I do, and I listen to Alistair Cooke's "Letter from America" with him.'

Their experience was quite different from that of another client I had, who told me that the only thing he and his ex-wife had had to agree about was that they both liked 'Coronation Street'.

Companionship need not mean always doing everything together. We ask our clients if they are prepared to take up new interests after they are married, and the majority usually are, but some cautiously add that it depends what the interests are.

Listening to a phone-in programme on the radio the other day I heard a woman holding forth about how she and her husband did everything together. On Saturdays they went to a supermarket and bought stores for the week. They kept the house clean together and did the gardening. They shared all each other's interests. The man answering the phone-in questions, just said, 'Umm — not everybody is the same, of course.'

The 'His and Hers' era came to Britain from America in the sixties. It seemed to start with embroidered bath towels and end up with men and women wearing the same T-shirts, jeans, length of hair and jewellery.

The present trend seems to be for women to be dashing and feminine, they can wear anything from sporting clothes to soft floating and silky ones. Real silk petticoats, cami-knickers, and nightdresses embroidered with lace are fashionable though expensive; and long suspenders and stockings rather than tights are considered most sexy. Unisex seems to have vanished, and it is considered all right again to have a few different interests from one's life partner. In many young families one parent takes a night off each week to pursue some particular interest and babysits for the other parent on another evening.

This I think is a much healthier relationship than the more stifling one of sharing everything. Both can be people in their own right and contribute something fresh to the marriage.

7 Finance

*Prosperity is not without many fears
and distastes; and adversity is not
without comfort and hope.*

FRANCIS BACON

Many of the worst quarrels between married couples are about money. In some families they can last for the whole of married life, and possibly even after death.

Until the Married Woman's Property Act of 1870 women had little or no control even over their dowries, and only the strong-minded ones had much to say about how they were provided for. Bess of Hardwick, a most formidable woman who lived in the sixteenth century when wives were looked upon as their husbands' property, was born into a fairly humble family. She managed to survive four husbands, administer their estates and become one of the richest women in England. Other women less shrewd or not so capable had to use other methods. The wife of a Scottish nobleman who lived in the Border Country used to have the dish on which the roast was served put before her husband for him to carve. If the larder was bare all he found when he lifted the cover was a pair of spurs. This was a hint that he should go over the border and bring back some English sheep and cattle.

If husbands and wives are bad providers or managers the family is bound to suffer and there will always be rows about each other's deficiencies. The other chief causes of disputes are extravagance, dependence, and meanness.

Extravagance can be a disease. One of my clients told me that his wife was a compulsive backer of horses. She spent most of the day working out the form and the rest of it backing losers. On the rare occasions when she had a winner it was almost worse, because she would then spend out on luxuries that, despite the winnings, they could not afford. Even now that they were divorced he still had to send her the occasional cheque to get her out of trouble.

A woman told me that her husband's two passions were clubs and cars. With school bills unpaid he would play bridge or backgammon for high stakes at one or other of his various clubs, and drive down to see their children in their respective schools in the newest model of expensive sports car. This did not go unnoticed by their headmasters who would shortly afterwards demand immediate payment — or else.

Dependence can be a problem too, particularly if the person with the money uses it as a power weapon. It can be a form of bullying. The marriage partner who is totally dependent on the husband or wife, whether rich or poor, and has to account for every penny, is in an unenviable position. In low-income families it is often impossible to allocate a definite sum that the husband or wife can spend as they wish. They cannot help but live a hand-to-mouth existence hoping that some extra expense doesn't strike them. If they are frank with each other they can plan together how to spend the money that they have. This is much better than one partner trying to carry the whole burden alone.

Amongst the richer husbands and wives a financial dependence can work satisfactorily, provided that the one without the money knows exactly how he or she stands. If a woman marries a man with less money than herself it is essential that they have an agreement about how he can keep up with her standard of living. If he cannot do it on his own resources and she refuses him the means to do so he is put in a difficult position. This applies equally to a wife who should, it seems to me, be given a definite allowance. A girl who came to see us after she had had a divorce from a rich man told us that she had left him after only few months of marriage. The reason was that he gave her money only after she slept with him, and then the amount varied according to how much he had enjoyed himself. When she left she advised him to marry a prostitute next time.

On the other hand, we heard from a divorced man that, in his opinion, his ex-wife behaved like a prostitute. She was extravagant and if she overspent her allowance and wanted something—usually clothes or jewellery—she would not allow him to make love to her unless he bought them. He had been very much in love with her and at first had thought this behaviour feminine and attractive. After a few years she became more and more materially demanding and eventually disgusted him so much that he stopped sleeping with her at all. He added that he was happy to say she had run off with another man.

Meanness on a small scale can be mildly irritating or even endearing, but it is slightly dotty. One man I know used to annoy his wife by saving string, painstakingly untying the knots on parcels they received, however small. He also believed that every bit of food in the kitchen could be used up if only his wife would put her mind to it. 'If he found a caterpillar in his salad he would expect me to cook it,' she once said. In other money matters he behaved perfectly rationally.

Clarissa and her first husband were friends of mine. He had died young and left her quite well off. Through us she later married another rich man who had a lovely house in the country. One day when she was in London she asked me out to lunch. She looked marvellous and radiated happiness, but she did tell me, as a joke, of her husband's idiosyncracy. He liked to entertain their friends and give them the best possible food and wine; he also gave her expensive presents and took her on marvellous holidays abroad. The only thing that he would not offer his guests or her were cigarettes, although he smoked himself. If she asked him for one he would give it to her, but a look of annoyance would flash across his face. She had asked him about this and he simply could not explain it. He knew that it was completely irrational. Now, she said, she always bought the cigarettes for their guests herself, and far from minding he even handed them round.

On a large scale meanness is a disease—a form of madness. Hilary came to see me because she wanted to marry to get away from home. She said that she was eighteen, but looked much younger and during our conversation she admitted that she was only sixteen. Her father had a good position in a large firm, but refused to spend money on his home. They had few labour-saving devices. Her mother never stood up for herself and only occasionally for her children. Hilary described her as looking old and washed out. It was obvious that she felt no sympathy for her and disliked both her parents. Her brothers, who at one time staged a rebellion, were told by their father that he was saving the money to leave to them. The eldest boy pointed out that as the father was only in his fifties they might not get the money for another forty years, and by that time it might not be worth much anyway. Shortly afterwards he left home, and her second brother was planning to do the same thing as soon as he could. I gave her a lecture about the stupidity of marrying simply to get away from home and, as she had no other idea of how to earn a living, advised her to ring up her Employment Exchange and ask them who was the nearest careers officer who would give help to people of her age.

Hilary, I hope, will get a job and leave home in the same way as her brother has done. Her father's meanness has ruined their whole family life.

In the early days of the Bureau women were not as independent as they are now and only a very few earned good incomes. Now we have many more women earning high salaries and doing what used to be known as men's jobs. A woman of twenty-eight answering a question on whether she was good with money replied, 'I have managed my own home successfully for four years, and budget my income.'

Many girls have their own houses or flats, bought or mortgaged, and have been responsible for their own finances for years and they sometimes have a grudge against the distinctions made between sons and daughters. Ann came from a well-known business family. Her brother automatically went into the family firm and never had to make much effort. She had worked hard to obtain an engineering degree and now earned a good salary. She was furious to find after her father died that not only had she been left less money in his will than her brother, but that it was tied up so that she did not have full control over it. When she went to see her solicitor about this he further angered her by saying, 'After all you might marry a rich man.'

When girls like this marry they will normally expect to share the living expenses with their husbands. Sometimes they have joint accounts, or they may decide that each should pay for specific things. If they have children they will plan for that too. If a woman gives up her work to look after them until they reach school age, she loses experience and seniority; on the other hand, if she goes to work she may well find that nurses and mothers' helps are difficult to get and expensive, and there are often domestic crises which cannot be planned for, but a determined woman will usually get by. This is a new problem for the middle-income groups. Lower-income mothers have often had to manage somehow, while higher-income women could afford to pay people to look after their children.

Although women who earn good money will nearly always insist that they want their husbands to earn as much or more than they do, husbands rarely ask for this. A nice thirty-year-old professional man wrote on his form, 'The way things are going it will be increasingly difficult to support a family. Some sort of earned income would be useful, but I cannot put a figure on this. It sounds too much like a business deal.'

Comparatively untrained women now earn much better salaries than they used to. Some secretaries are ambitious and use their jobs as a stepping stone to big business. Others do not want careers. Sally — our feather-headed blonde — was the secretary to a doctor when she first came to us. I often wonder if he still has a practice as she said that the urgent calls that came through upset her so much that she would become confused. She later became a receptionist to a specialist, which she found more peaceful. His hours were regular, many of them spent at the hospital, and appointments with him were made by doctors rather than the patients themselves. The specialist, however, complained of the smell of nail polish, as Sally used to spend hours manicuring her nails to while away the time. She next thought of getting a job as a receptionist in an hotel, where she hoped it would be more lively. When I last spoke to her she had been tempted by another position, which she had seen advertised in the evening paper. It promised 'Central plush office! Tropical plants! No typing! Young Handsome Director!'

We have numbers of girls in this category — many of them more intelligent than Sally and earning more money, but without ambition. They want somewhere to live, possibly sharing with other people, and enough money for smart clothes. They are really marking time until they marry. Many of them are prepared to go on working after marriage, at any rate for a while. They will earn money to help buy extras for their home, and if they have children will probably stay at home and look after them. They will probably not go back to work when the children are off their hands, unless they are bored alone in their home, or it becomes financially necessary.

What is happening most markedly is that many of our

most prosperous British clients—both men and women—zoom in from abroad. The women, most of whom live on unearned incomes, come from such places as Spain, the Canary Islands, or the South of France, which can offer sunshine and British enclaves where they can make friends; quite a few come from the Channel Islands. However, the snag is that in all these places there is a superfluity of women.

Mrs Clifton-Smith, a very rich widow who wants to remarry, told me that she had thought of emigrating to one of these tax havens, but after having visited them all she decided that the ratio of men to women would be more in her favour in England. She is a dynamic and energetic woman: apart from running her beautiful house and garden on a third of the staff she should have, she has started a small factory in a local town which has become big business.

Many other women of Mrs Clifton-Smith's type remain in Britain because that is where their families and friends live. They are particularly apt to stay if they take part in local social or political activities, or have simply built up a good social life. Some of these women are amazing. One in her sixties is slim and beautiful; she hunts, plays golf, is well read and amusing and also very well off. I have not at the time of writing been able to take her on as a client because I have not got a man in the right age group who is good enough for her.

The men, most of whom are still in business, are more mobile; they write to us that they will be coming to England from America, Japan, Amsterdam, Geneva, the oil countries and other centres where international business is done on a big scale by Britons who do not like this country's high rate of taxation. One of them has a nostalgia for Gloucestershire, where he lived as a child, and would like to marry a woman from that part of the world. Another puts in long telephone calls from West Germany whenever he is coming to England and gives us the dates when he will be in a particular part of the country.

Ted who came in looking bronzed and fit works in the Middle East. He has a good tax-free income, a car, and an air-conditioned luxury flat thrown in. He was particularly interested in meeting a girl who would be good at giving parties. To use his own words, 'Entertaining is an integral part of life in the Arabian Gulf.' He enjoyed it. His reason for coming to us, he said, was because single girls were somewhat of a rarity in that part of the world.

A nurse who had also lived in the Middle East was not so enamoured of it. Where she was no woman was allowed to drive a car; a hospital mini-bus took them everywhere and although they didn't actually have to wear a yashmak, they were not allowed to go about with bare arms, and their dresses or shirts had to be buttoned right up to their necks. She said that the no alcohol law had been very strictly applied where she was and she had had no social life. The pay had been good and tax free, but she was delighted to be back in England.

It is interesting that this is happening. When we first started we had businessmen and tea-planters joining because their idea was to retire as soon as they had made enough money and come back to live in Britain. Now the men who have made the money are looking for wives from this country to share their exile from Britain.

This way of avoiding taxation is legal and sensible but I find it sad. It was during the war when we were fighting for freedom that our manners and our characters, it seems to me, changed for the worse. Before then money was rarely talked about in public: it was considered ill-bred and vulgar to do so. But as we tightened our belts so we talked. Over a meal of spam we would compare notes about its quality, its price and where it could be bought more cheaply. We also learnt to wangle. There was a black market for everything and even normally honest people used it in a small way.

They would buy a few yards of 'unrationed' material and also petrol coupons without asking questions. Mothers would buy sweet coupons or extra sugar for their children if they got the chance.

I lived in the country during part of the war and I remember being told by my office that if I could bring some onions and potatoes they might be able to get one of the office typewriters mended; and another time if I could bring up some bottled fruit they could get me some real wax furniture polish.

The forms that the government made us fill in multiplied, for private citizens as well as for businesses, and have been increasing in number and difficulty ever since. They are now so complicated that more and more people have to go to already overworked accountants and pay enormous fees to have what should be a simple matter sorted out. People use tax consultants to find ethical ways of paying as little income tax as possible, and anybody who does not claim all possible benefits and allowances from the government is looked upon as an imbecile.

This sort of attitude, together with the effects of the war which turned us into a paternalistic state, has undermined our feelings of responsibility and honesty. We find that our clients are much more dishonest about paying their after-marriage fees than they used to be, and this is just as true of people with plenty of money as of those with less.

We discovered one of the most blatant pieces of dishonesty when a furious woman rang us up and asked us how we had dared to introduce her son to a girl whom he had subsequently married without knowing that she was a divorcee. Neither the son's name nor the girl's name meant anything to us. We searched the files and all the cross-references we keep to no avail, and rang the mother back. Again we said that we had never heard of either her son or her daughter-in-law and asked her if she knew if he had paid his registration fee by cheque and if he had paid his after-marriage fee. There was a long pause. Then she said, 'I gave him the money in cash to join your bureau and did the same for their after-marriage fee.' She then added, 'It was such a quick marriage too.' We were very sorry for her as her son had obviously found this deception a splendid way of getting hold of a bit of quick cash, and had probably met the girl he wanted to marry sometime earlier.

Mr Parsons who tried to avoid paying our after-marriage fee was high up in what could be called one of the more responsible branches in the government services. He never let us know that he had become engaged, but neither he nor the girl had asked for any more introductions after they had met, nor had they replied to our letters. We eventually wrote a letter to the flat where she had lived asking for it to be forwarded if necessary. We got it back with 'Not Known' written on the envelope, but in her handwriting. We then rang the telephone exchange to ask if a new subscriber, Mr Parsons, had a number at that address and they gave it to us. We telephoned and got paid.

Another couple who married without telling us went to the Middle East. We had no replies from our letters addressed to his flat, but we obtained her forwarding address from her old firm. They paid, but wrote the most ungracious letter when they did so.

Another case was most extraordinary. One of my interviewers was staying with some friends in the country near an hotel famous for its comfort and good food. One evening she had dinner there and at the next table sat Major Field and Miss Young. Miss Young wore a brand new wedding ring and what looked like a large engagement ring. My interviewer had written to them a few weeks before asking them how they were getting on and if they wanted more introductions. They said that they didn't and would let us know if they became engaged. We were rather surprised in the office to get their after-marriage fee out of the blue a few days before the interviewer returned.

Other couples write and say that they cannot pay their after-marriage fee because they have had so many expenses getting married. These seem to include an expensive honeymoon, washing machine, and deep freeze. I sometimes rather sourly point out that as they bought them because they were married our fee should come first.

It seems to me that rather than being really dishonest this attitude stems from a new way of thinking. It is every man for himself. We are told by the government that we should claim all the allowances that we can get. And some of our clients feel that it is up to us to find out if they are married. If we don't that is just too bad; it is our fault.

Happily it is only a small number of clients who behave like this; most of them are thrilled and grateful when we get them married. Some in fact send the after-marriage fees as soon as they have arranged the date and before they have married.

Sometimes a couple will come into the office to say that they are engaged, often they are off to buy a ring in Bond Street, or sometimes the girl will proudly show us one that they have just bought.

One man who came into the office to pay his after-marriage fee found that the interviewer who had looked after him was out so he left a note. It said, 'Sorry to miss you. I just looked in to thank you for finding me a very nice wife. All well. I promised to embrace you if ever this happened, so it may be as well I have missed you.' The interviewer to whom he'd given the note just scribbled on the piece of paper, 'Oh, oh. Sweet man, he really wanted to see you personally and thank you.'

8 Religion

Silent and amazed even when a little boy,
I remember I heard the preacher every Sunday put
God in his statements,
As against some being or influence.

WALT WHITMAN

When our clients come to see us they do not on the whole talk much about their religion. They will say if they are practising or non-practising and what beliefs they want their husband or wife to hold, but not a great deal more.

In the thirties my clients of all denominations were more under the influence of their families as regards religion. I had one client, called Jonathan, whose family held morning prayers which every member of the household was expected to attend. This was quite a common habit then, but Jonathan said that every time he asked a girl friend home to stay it led to trouble. Either she did not get up in time to join in, or she could not be persuaded that he was merely conforming to his parents' wishes by being there. She would not believe he would not continue the custom when he inherited the estate.

Today, if clients say that they belong to a religion they mean it. Their beliefs may not be the same as those of their families. Quite a few of them take up cults from other countries such as Yoga, Zen-Buddhism, or those involving meditation.

More recently founded institutions, the Jehovah's Witnesses which started in 1872, and Scientology which reached England in the 1950s, have come from America and seem harsh. Several of my clients have told me how their marriages have been broken up by them. One man who was a captain in the army said that his wife became a Jehovah's Witness. She left him because members of that sect were not allowed to serve in the armed forces or to salute a national flag, so she felt that they were incompatible. A woman whose husband became a Scientologist told me that he left her and their three children because she would not become one. He went to live in another country and pays nothing towards the children's support. He now calls himself 'The Reverend'.

The Church of England is tolerant about mixed marriages and does not stipulate in which religion the children of these marriages should be brought up. The day when divorced people can remarry in church seems to be getting nearer. Roman Catholics, however, are still insistent that children of a mixed marriage should be brought up in that religion. In spite of this we get quite a number of Catholics who say that if they married outside their Church they would be open-minded about this.

Christopher, who called himself a non-practising Roman Catholic, said just that. He was in his thirties, very good-looking, and earning a lot of money. He wanted to meet a girl from a good background, which when I probed further I gathered meant a good financial one. We always point out in these cases that, although the client may not mind which Church their children are christened in, their families may. He assured me that his family would not mind and got engaged to a Protestant. Then his grandmother whom he had never looked upon as being a very active Roman Catholic said she would not leave him her money if he failed to bring his children up as Catholics. To make sure he did so the girl was to become a convert before they married. This the girl refused to do, saying it would be hypocritical, and the engagement was broken off.

We also get Roman Catholics who have been divorced. One, an Irishman who can at times be very amusing, becomes quite bitter and irrational on the subject, and in self-defence refuses to meet any other Roman Catholic, divorced or not.

In 1968 I opened a Jewish branch of the Bureau in London and I now have one in Leeds as well. Both interviewers are of the Faith, the strictly Orthodox members of which obey stringent rules. They fast at certain times and eat only Kosher food. A man will not shake hands with a woman, will always have his head covered, in and outside the house, will wear a beard, always wash his hands before eating, and sleep with a pitcher of water within easy each. The Orthodox woman will shave her head when she is married and wear a wig or *shaytlin* to make her less attractive to other men. She is not allowed to wear men's clothing. One of our young Orthodox Jews was upset when we introduced him to a girl who was Orthodox too, but she was wearing trousers. As it is only children born of a Jewish mother who are of the Faith it is important for the family that their sons marry Jewish wives.

The Jews have a very strong family sense and parents often make the first contact with us on behalf of their children. When they do we always point out that if we help their son or daughter it must be with their consent. My interviewers say, however, that there is now much less pressure from the family. The clients themselves are not so interested as to whether they marry Separdi or Ashknazi as they were even in 1968. Some of them say that they are not interested in religion.

In England the law neither encourages nor discourages religions as it once used to do. The state is paternalistic and has taken away a lot of authority from parents and with it family feeling. We now live in a materialistic world and need spiritual thought and ideals to counter this. Yet the churches are emptying. As one of my clients said, 'My parents were happy and secure in their religion even when dying. I only wish I could feel the same.'

9 Class

Snobbishness sometimes is thought to be a prerogative of the rich. But no man is so poverty-stricken he can't afford to be a snob.

HAL BOYLE, ASSOCIATED PRESS

Today class is much less important to our clients than it was when I first started the Bureau. Then we used to listen to long tales about the grandeur of their ancestors and relations. Now, certainly amongst the younger clients, we do not.

Except for Royalty no hereditary titles have been created in Britain since 1955. Both Princess Anne's and Princess Alexandra's husbands have kept their original status. If this trend continues it means that it is only a matter of time before there will be no titles except, perhaps, for the Royal Family. For political reasons, to stay in the House of Commons rather than be moved to the Lords, several peers have renounced their peerages, and one or two, like John Siddley (Lord Kenilworth), the interior decorator, and Patrick Campbell (Lord Glenavy), the writer and television personality, do not use their titles for their work. Knighthoods once awarded to brave young men on the battlefield are now given as a reward for long and faithful service. The same applies to life peerages, so a title is often associated with old age.

English aristocracy was never like the French who would put up with hideous discomfort just to be near the king at Versailles in the hope of advancing their ambitions. During the last hundred years the court has kept a low profile and most people would be hard put to it to name any of the present courtiers. Britain has an aristocracy who, on the whole, prefer the country to the town and work hard to keep up enormous houses, palaces and castles. They compete against each other with their entertainments, such as zoos, museums and pop festivals; and a number of them offer visitors expensive weekends as guests in their homes. Most of them are fighting a losing battle against taxation, death duties, and the uphill task of keeping the place propped up. How much longer their descendants will be dedicated enough to go on trying, and if they do what ruses they will think up to keep themselves solvent, remains to be seen. Rich heiresses are no longer as anxious to take on the properties with the title as they were in the old days. Many beautiful homes now belong to the nation, and we must hope that if other owners give up their stately homes the nation will take them over.

The great families are still something of a club. For generations they have intermarried. The boys have gone to the same schools as their fathers, and the girls, who were taught by governesses at home, made friends only from the circle chosen for them by their parents. Now they have more freedom in that they too go to boarding schools, but they still stay pretty much with their own kind.

We always ask our clients about their relationships with their families and most of them seem to be good, if a bit casual. One or two clients who have 'bettered' themselves have deliberately cut adrift because they are ashamed of or, as they usually put it, bored with, their background. This I always find sad, but fortunately rare. On one or two occasions, though, I have been astounded. One woman who was a cook told me that she went on her holiday to Southsea and there sitting on the beach next to her was a man who reminded her strongly of her father whom she had not seen or heard of for twenty years. He kept looking at her too and they spoke to each other and found out that indeed he was her father. She had travelled from job to job and so had he. They were neither of them well educated and since writing was not easy for them, they had simply lost touch. Recently I heard an urgent message given out on the radio for the parents of a man who was dangerously ill in hospital. They gave the last-known address of the parents but they had left there three years ago. This sort of situation happens much more to families who have no land; small farmers, smallholders, and cottagers, as well as the landed gentry, have often lived in the same place for hundreds of years. There is much less continuity in the large towns and suburbs that have grown up, and it is much easier to get lost.

Amongst our upper- and middle-class clients it is the older ones who are the most snobbish. Mrs Treble-Barrelled — she managed to have two hyphens to her surname — said that she must meet a man who had been to a good public school. She refused to meet the man to whom I offered to introduce her because his school had been a minor one. She was most upset when, sending her another introduction, I explained that the first man's father had not had much money but had been the third son of an earl. She wrote back by return to say that that was different, but by then the man had written to say he was getting engaged to another client to whom we had introduced him.

One woman whom we asked to come for an interview was furious and said that only servants were interviewed. She enclosed a photograph of herself taken at Ascot.

Nancy Mitford in her article in the 1950s about U and non-U made the situation worse for some people. They got really worried if they had been saying 'note paper' when all the time they should have been saying 'writing paper'.

A good-looking and amusing man in his early sixties wrote to us and said, 'I don't know what you thought of me at the interview but please don't introduce me to the "pardon and toilet" brigade.' Others in that age group ask for people with good backgrounds — not described — and people who are 'ladies' or 'gentlemen'. The fine points of gentility which are roused sometimes take us by surprise.

One promising friendship was broken off because one of the two said 'table napkin' and the other 'serviette'.

Younger people are not only less concerned about such matters but some of them are very much against the 'posh' accents of their parents, and their class distinctions. Anne who came from a good upper-class family was clever and had been to a university. She didn't mind about class: she wanted brains and somebody determined to use them and to get on. We took her at her word and introduced her to a man who had gone to university by winning scholarships and had got a good degree. Anne's mother and father liked him, but were worried about his family's antagonism. His parents were simple people who had been horrified rather than proud of his career so far, and they were now bristling with rage. They said that Anne was not the sort of girl who had been brought up to look after a husband properly, and she would hamper his career. What finally nearly wrecked the wedding was the insistence by the bride's father that he and his friends would wear morning coats, and the bride-groom's equally firm insistence that he and his friends would not. Anne described the wedding guests to me as looking rather like the Roundheads and Cavaliers drawn up for battle, the two sides wore different sorts of clothes and never mixed. However, her marriage is happy and they have three lovely children. The in-laws meet only at the christenings.

Georgina was very pretty and beautifully turned out. She had well-tinted and beautifully cut blonde hair which fell perfectly into place. Her make-up was flawless, and her nails exactly the colour to complement it, and she wore just the right amount of expensive gold chains, bracelets and rings. Most people when I am interviewing them and going through the form that they have filled in, lean back in their chairs; she leant over the desk and went over the form too, sometimes explaining a point before I got to it. I gathered that her parents had a nice house in the country and had let her have a flat in Chelsea. She obviously had quite a good brain but did not want to be a worker: she wanted to do something spectacular, easy and profitable. She said that she had very nearly been on to several 'big deals' — she never explained what they were — but none of them had got off the ground. For the last few years she had been a sort of super personal assistant and office manager to a young man called Ron with whom she had had an affair. She didn't get much salary, but was going to get a good lump sum when things really came off. When I asked her what Ron did she said he was into all kinds of things. He was a sort of trader and supplier and at the moment he was 'into boats'. This translated meant that he bought old yachts and did them up to charter out. He had even tried to get hold of an old liner for cruises. The money hadn't rolled in and he had once admitted that his family had had to help him out. He never talked about his family otherwise and she did not know where they lived.

I asked her what had happened to Ron and she said that at first she had been attracted to him because he was unlike anybody she had ever met before. She had built him up to her family as being a major tycoon and then when they asked her to bring him down to stay she had got cold feet and had not even told Ron about the invitation. She could hear her father asking him penetrating questions about his business and summing him up as a phoney. Then her mother asked her if she would mind if she sold her tiara. Her mother had worn it at her wedding and so had her grand-mother, and Georgina knew that it had been kept for hers. 'This,' she said, 'brought it home to me that I was getting on and ought to get married. I really wasn't getting anywhere or having a particularly good or interesting time. A lot of night clubs but that was about all.' She wanted somebody not too conventional, who liked winter sports, holidays in the sun and getting as much fun out of life as possible.

The real class difficulty that we have amongst the younger clients is between blue- and white-collar workers. Many girls from blue-collar families become secretaries and turn white collar, and they are then reluctant to marry back into blue. We have at the moment a young man who works with his hands, and they show the marks of it. He is rugged rather than good looking, strongly built, quiet voiced, and extremely nice. He earns a good salary in a business which he and his father work in together; he has a Porsche but prefers to ride his motor bike. It is not easy to find the right sort of girl for him, so many of them prefer somebody with a nine to six job in an office and if they are lucky a small car. A few girls are beginning to see what is happening. Not only are the blue-collar workers earning more money than the white, but often they are just as well educated and have a higher standard of living.

The big money spenders are forming an altogether different class. They are not winning their houses and possessions by fighting wars, but by making money. They can come from nowhere and disappear again as quickly, or else establish their money dynasties. The new hierarchy upsets some of the older generation who since their youth have been used to having special treatment. One of my clients told me that her grandfather had taken her to an hotel for lunch recently and had not been given the table he expected. Worse than that, the room had been rearranged so that a bigger party could have it. 'His face puckered like a spoilt baby's,' she told me, and then he said, 'Nobody seems to care about people like me any more.'

He was quite right, we are living in a commercial age and competition is keen. Things are changing, and they always will change; it would be unhealthy if they did not. In any age and under any regime there always has been and always will be an élite. People revel in or dislike the changes depending on whether they are leading successful lives or not.

10 Why Marry?

*Everything that lives, lives not alone
nor to itself.*

WILLIAM BLAKE

Swinging London was at its height in the late fifties and the early sixties. It catered for youth. They wore mini-skirts, put their vertebrae out of place with the Hula Hoop, and performed prodigious athletic feats doing the Twist. It was all good fun.

The Permissive Age followed. Any age group could join in. Morals were changing, and the fact was being advertised. Many people said that this was the end of marriage. Why should anybody bother to marry if they could sleep with whomsoever they wanted, have children without divulging whose they were, and live in communes where everything and everybody could be shared? In spite of these forebodings marriage goes on.

The fact is that most European countries have always been monogamous. As Westermark points out in his *History of Marriage* monogamy had nothing to do with Christianity. The Greeks and Latins were monogamous before the time of Christ. The exceptions seem to have been an occasional Irish chieftain and the Merovingian kings, who were the rulers of the Franks in the fifth century. Charlemagne was the last French king to follow their example. In many other parts of the world polygamy is accepted and rich men have harems. In very poor countries it can be the custom for several men to share and support one wife and her children. Matriarchy was somewhat different from this because the real power often rested with the matriarch's nearest or perhaps most powerful male relative. Whichever system these men and women lived under they had to keep the rules, otherwise they would have been punished by ostracism or death.

London today seems effete and scruffy rather than swinging, and there is no particular reason to be permissive as most things are allowed. The Law has become much more benevolent: people may marry at eighteen, and get an inexpensive divorce, provided both parties want it. One hopes that illegitimacy will be abolished, too. The effect of the new freedoms has not yet been fully felt, but I think that with man's natural wish for law and order the gentler rules will help towards more thoughtful and happier marriages.

Mating is a survival instinct and often a pleasure. Human beings like to make rules about it. They like to commit themselves to somebody or something even if they can't keep to the high standards that they intended. During the marriage ceremony they will promise in good faith to love and cherish each other in sickness and in health for ever. Sometimes they are not strong enough to fulfil their good intentions.

My younger clients often used to say, 'I don't want to belong to the Permissive Age.' They seemed to think that marriage was going to be abolished and they didn't want that. One girl, looking at me with large doe-like eyes, said, 'I have a feeling of insecurity. I always imagined that I would marry and have children and then grandchildren, and have continuity in my family life, but that seems to be dying out.'

Many of my clients have told me that at one time they thought that marriage was unnecessary, old fashioned and expensive. Philip, who had been living with a girl, recounted: 'We decided that we would make our promises to each other in private, and that we would stay together for ever. After three years she decided that she was going to live with another man. She was sorry, she said, but even with the best intentions people made mistakes.'

Liza—a very feminine girl who should have married

young and had babies—lived with a man for several years, hoping that he would eventually marry her. He had said that as they loved each other so much they did not have to make special promises. She started a baby hoping to make him change his mind, but he made her have an abortion. She ended by saying quietly, 'Afterwards I was glad that this had happened. He didn't love me enough to marry me and he wouldn't have loved our child.'

When my interviewer asked Dennis if he was free to marry he looked desperate. 'I'm not married,' he said, 'but I'm living with a girl and I can't get rid of her.' Advising him to follow the old adage and be off with the old love before he was on with the new, we said that we could not take him on until he had sorted himself out.

Margaret told me about a man who wanted her to live with him. They would go through the marriage service together, in private, and make the promises to each other. She asked him why they would be more likely to keep the promises they made in private than the ones they made in public. Whereupon he flew into a rage and said, 'You just want to show off at a big wedding.' As it happened that was the last thing she wanted, and she left him because she did not think that he was genuinely fond of her. She added wryly that he found a replacement for her very quickly.

We do get a lot of people who are separated wanting to become clients. Talking to one on the telephone I said, 'We can't take you until you have your absolute, but what's the hurry? Take your time, go out with people, but don't commit yourself or make rash promises until you are free.' A few months later he rang back. 'I just want to thank you,' he **said**, 'we've made it up and are no longer separated, thank you for putting some sense into me.'

Loneliness is not the best reason for getting married. If a man or a woman has plenty of friends but needs a deeper relationship marriage may be the answer. If he or she just needs a prop it can be dangerous.

Two girls came in to see us on the same day. Elizabeth was likable, good tempered, extroverted and energetic. She told me that she had lots of boy friends, and had several times been on the brink of becoming engaged, but there had always been something lacking. She supposed that she hadn't been in love for she had never had a feeling of oneness. She would like somebody in whom she could confide her hopes and fears, somebody she could trust and with whom she could share her life. She said that she noticed some couples who although apparently happily married seemed to be lonely.

Penny was the opposite. She said that she was shy, and she was certainly self-pitying. Night after night she sat alone, doing nothing, and often she did not go on holiday because she had nobody to go with; instead she went and stayed with her parents, which she did not count as a holiday, she said, because it was so boring. She was anything but shy with me because she was so forthcoming about her woes. No man, I told her, was likely to find her interesting in her present state of mind. I suggested that she took up a few outside interests, if she went to her local library, town hall or church, or scanned the papers, she would find that there were many activities such as amateur dramatics, music societies, sightseeing walks, badminton, etc, which would not be expensive and where she would see other people.

Funnily enough Penny got engaged before Elizabeth did. Elizabeth liked and was well liked by most of the people whom she met so it took her some time to sort out her feelings. It was nearly two years before she married. Penny was engaged within a few months. The man was rather older than she had asked for. I think he wanted to give her the protection that she felt she needed.

In the thirties it was accepted that women would be dependent on men. Clever women accepted this but managed to get their own way.

One man told me that his ex-wife Susie, a tiny and

appealing blonde, had had one of the most calculating brains of anybody that he had ever met, and, in his own words, 'could have acted Sarah Bernhardt right off the stage.' She had no money herself but managed to obtain a great deal from him, and somehow always made it appear that he was in the wrong. A few years after they were married she said to another woman in front of some of their friends, 'What a lovely ring you are wearing. My engagement ring was like that, but I had to get rid of it.' Warming to her subject, he said, she even managed to produce a tear. His friends looked accusingly at him as if he had been keeping her short of housekeeping money, and only later when he forced her to explain did he find out that she had pawned some of the jewellery he had given her to subsidise her ample dress allowance. He always thought that she was marvellously well dressed and if ever he asked her where she had bought any of her clothes she would reply, 'Oh, at a little shop I found,' without naming it, for fear he would know that it was one of the most expensive in London. She eventually ran off with a friend of his. The friend had a beautiful Bentley, but not long after she'd left he met the friend at a bus stop. 'What's happened to your car?' he asked. 'Susie always wants it now,' his friend replied gloomily, 'I hardly ever drive it.'

It is less common for people to come to us and say that they want to marry for money than it used to be. If they do, it is often because they have been used to having money and simply want to live in the way in which they are accustomed. A girl who earns a good income will want to live comfortably. The most difficult cases are the older people on fixed incomes which are diminishing in purchasing power every year. They often feel that they must marry for money. We get very few obvious fortune hunters and if we do and we see no reason why they should marry someone with a lot of money we simply tell them that we have nobody for them at the moment.

Now that the mercenary dependence of the thirties has, on the whole, gone, other dependences show up. The poor weak woman can still wreck havoc with the strong man. A mental dependence is often an attraction too.

A man came to see me saying that he wanted to get married. His mother, whom he admired and loved, had been left a widow. She had taken up a career and been a success, but she had been over-protective and had dominated him. He was in his twenties and had a good job as an accountant in a large publishing firm. He wanted to meet a non-career girl who was not likely to become a tycoon.

Finally he met Clara. She had not only had a dominating mother, but a brilliant elder brother, and apparently few brains of her own. She told me that she had finished her education at a famous university town, implying that she had been at the university. Actually she had been at a school there, where she had studied drama and begun a secretarial course. She didn't really want to work; she wanted to have her own home and children.

Their first meeting went off well. They walked round Kew Gardens which was near to where she lived. He then dropped her home and she suggested that he came in for a cup of tea. They were alone in the house and while she made the tea he was left in the drawing room. When she came back he was looking at the books in a small bookcase, the only one they had in the room. An avid reader himself he was surprised at how few books there were, and was even more surprised when she said, 'We don't have many books, only those written by our friends.' He glanced at the bookcase again — Jane Austen, Galsworthy and Dickens seemed to be the principal authors. He told me later that he fell in love with her at that moment. She had tried to impress him as she had tried to impress me, but she had not got the weapons to do it. He felt protective towards her.

Over half the clients who come to us now have been

married before. Men or women whose partners have died have a tendency to think of them as near perfect. Losing their companionship they remember their marriage as being more ideal than it was. It is perhaps a form of compensation that we remember the best things about people whom we have loved and who have died. But if clients talk excessively about their late spouse we suggest that it might make it difficult for their future partner and advise them to wait a little longer before they remarry. We feel much more comfortable when a man or a woman says that he or she was happily married and would like to be so again.

The reactions of people who have been divorced are more varied. A great many people looking back calmly once all the heat has gone out of the separation think that their marriage might have been happy but for some quite minor fault in either or both of them.

Charles, an amiable looking thirty-five-year-old, told me that he and his wife got divorced because they had such terrible quarrels. 'We were so nearly right for each other,' he said. 'I'm not naturally aggressive, but if she scored a verbal point I felt that I had to go one better. She's perfectly happily married now to a man who when she starts to shout at him simply laughs at her. Apparently she hardly ever shouts now.'

Gerald, lean, sexy looking and, I would think, inclined to have a wandering eye, said, 'I had so many home truths told to me during my marriage that it has taken me time to digest them. She was right over some things. I was certainly selfish and thoughtless in many ways.' He paused, and then he added, 'She was frightful at times, too. I hope she's taken in some of the things I told her. If we'd both done so we'd probably be still together.'

Bella when she came to see us was still furious that her husband had left her. Her attitude—which she scarcely bothered to cover up—was 'I'll show him'. She wanted somebody better looking, more successful, and richer. Her husband had deserted her for a much younger girl so at least she had not been hurt in the way that some women are by his leaving her for somebody older. This is a terrible blow to a younger and pretty woman, more so if the other woman is plain.

Some people will never learn. They fall madly in love and marry and then fall madly out of love again. Men often stick to the same type when they do this. One or two friends of mine have, when they remarried, chosen a bride younger but similar to the last.

Women do not seem to go for the same type so much. In fact they will often say that they would like someone opposite in both looks and character to their ex-husband.

I have met people socially who, knowing that I run the Marriage Bureau, have said belligerently, 'I will never get married', or, as the case may be, 'remarried'. My invariable reply is that it is optional; nobody should get married unless they want to.

Women have always been much more brainwashed into getting married than men have and it has made them more humble. A man of forty-eight — attractive and prosperous — told us not long ago that he had not married before because he had not wished to do so. Women up to their mid-thirties may now give us this reason, but single women over that age group are generally much less confident.

This brainwashing is not so much in evidence today, but we do occasionally get men or women coming along either because they have been talked into the idea, or because they have been married before and miss the state of being married rather than the actual husband or wife.

Two women in their forties joined us at the same time. They had both been married before and had grown-up children. Molly, the driving force, had persuaded her friend Elsa to come. They were interviewed by different staff, but on comparing their forms we could see that Molly really wanted marriage so would be much easier to help than Elsa who was not so genuinely keen. She was just lonely.

Molly worked for a well-known charity and had a busy life. She was practising Church of England herself, but did not mind what, if any, religious opinions her husband had. She gave us a wide age range, and did not expect her husband to support her entirely. She was prepared to travel and live abroad and did not really mind about height and personal appearance; she said that it depended on the man. She did not mind if he was divorced, or if he had children, provided they were teenagers or over. Elsa made many stipulations. The man had to hold the same religious views as herself, be the same age or only a few years older, tall, and preferably not divorced. She did not want any children who lived at home. He must have a nice house, and although she had more money than Molly she did not seem to be prepared to give much help financially. She had few interests. My interviewer told her that she could only meet a very few people if she joined, which made her indignant, and in fact she chose not to join.

Most people come to a point in their lives when they want to marry, some more than once. Molly had been happily married before, and wanted to be again. We were sure that she would make a good job of it. She was liked by every man she met, and remarried again eighteen months later. She was the marrying kind.

11 Why People come to the Marriage Bureau

Walking home late, watched by all manner of things but
by nothing human; tree barks glowing,
almost rain falling. My friends in all cities,
in Liverpool, in London phoning
maybe living perhaps
Wondering what to do this evening.

BRIAN PATTEN

I answered the telephone the other morning and a man of eighteen asked me if I could find him a wife. I said that it would be difficult as the women we had in his age group were looking for somebody slightly older. I then asked him if he was living away from home. This is usually the case when men of his age contact me. They miss the company at home and its comforts so want a home of their own. To my surprise his case was different. He was living at home, but wanted to get away.

This request made me think how much things had changed during the forty years that I have been running the Marriage Bureau. In the thirties and forties it was the girls who needed marriage as an escape from their parents. As at that time, if under twenty-one they could not marry without their parents' consent and we rarely took them on until they had reached that age. If we did, we made sure that their parents had approved of their coming to us.

Now that the law has changed, men are marrying much younger, many of them in their late teens. The tragic announcements of the deaths of young soldiers, such as those stationed in Northern Ireland, in their early twenties, married and with children, emphasises this fact.

Speaking generally, girls in their early teens grow up more

quickly than boys, and for that reason when it comes to marriage want to meet a man a few years older than themselves. Such a man is also likely to be earning a better living and to be more settled in his career.

When the Marriage Bureau first started the principal reasons people came to me were unequal distribution of the sexes, smaller families, and lack of money. Some of the unequal distribution was because we then had an Empire and lots of eligible men left Britain to earn their living there. Also, men were crowding into big towns, because that was where the money was. Smaller families meant there was less opportunity to meet husbands or wives through brothers and sisters and their friends; and for many people money was tight, so there was less entertaining.

After the war Mayfair and its debs changed. There were still lists of deb dances and cocktail parties in *The Times*, and some families did almost anything to get themselves into the glossies. Young men, mostly those who had been to the right schools and were on 'The List', received shoals of invitations from people they did not know. One or two young men, especially if they had not been to the right school, managed to do quite well being paid by fathers not to marry their daughters. It was quite a profitable trade.

In the early fifties when the whole coming-out industry had become commercialised and was rather on the wane, I had a flat in London and shared a party telephone line with Lady X., who augmented her income by having debutantes to stay in her house for the season. My only hope, if the telephone was engaged, which it nearly always was since there were several girls using it, as well as Lady X. busily fixing up their social life, was to wait until they had finished their conversation, slam down the receiver and dial at once. This way I heard a number of boring conversations, but some quite funny ones too. One girl's mother, whose voice I recognised by the slight North Country accent, used to telephone every morning for an exact account of what her daughter had been doing the night before: where she had been; whom she had danced with; who else had been in the party, etc. She was clearly checking up to see that she was getting her money's worth.

Lady X. could be pretty forthright. In answer to an enquiry from a friend as to who a certain girl was, she replied, 'Nobody. She just went to Y', Y being a well-known and snobbish girls' school.

Coming-out became a farce, and many girls refused to take part in it. Presentations at court stopped in 1958 which furthered its decline. A wan little list of cocktail parties, and an occasional small dance—often given by one or more mothers—is still published. Really big coming-out dances are rare. Pictures in the glossies of girls who are 'coming-out' now have rather apologetic captions saying that the girls are studying something or other, rather like the asinine conversations conducted during the 'Miss World' contest which are intended to bring out the girls' personalities. I would love to see a picture of a deb underneath which was written 'I am coming out to have as good a time as possible, meet people useful to my social life, and collect as many boy friends as I can.'

Mothers who had looked forward to their daughters' doing a season were getting worried. In the 1960s one said to me, 'Susan refuses to come out. She just wants to live in Chelsea. She's not meeting any of the right people. Do you think you could help?' In that case we couldn't. Susan never came near us. She was probably in love with one of the 'wrong' people.

Many parents were relieved that things had changed, especially mothers who had dreaded the thought of going to the numerous luncheons that were required attendance if they wanted to ensure that their daughters were invited to the right dances and that the right people came to theirs. Fathers, too, thought happily about the enormous cheques that they would not have to sign.

Some girls became neither one thing nor the other. Pat, who had been a reluctant sort of semi-deb, had not enjoyed it and after the season was over sat about at home saying that she wanted to go to London and do something creative. This infuriated her father, who said impatiently that, as she had no talent, the best way for her to be creative was for her to get married and have children. Thinking it over she agreed, became one of our clients and did just that.

Samantha's father gave her a choice. He told her that she could have a coming-out dance if she liked but, as an alternative, he offered her a trip round the world. She chose to travel because she thought that she might never have the chance again. She never regretted it, but developed a wanderlust. She became an air hostess and, when that began to pall, a glorified mother's help in America. There she was paid an enormous salary and given her own car. When she came to us she stipulated that the man she married should have the sort of job which would entail living abroad. When I last heard from her she and her husband were living in Hong Kong.

Clare found life in the country boring. She lived in the home counties and it was all right at weekends when people of her generation came back from London — bringing piles of laundry to be washed and leaving with piles of food as their mothers were sure they weren't eating properly. During the week there seemed to be few unmarried contemporaries around. She persuaded her parents to allow her to live in London and take a secretarial course. She left her comfortable home to live in comparative squalor with an old school friend and another girl. When she came to see me she said, 'It's pretty awful.' She did not mean the squalor. She did not like the secretarial college and was bad at it, and in the flat she was very much the odd one out. One girl was engaged so was out practically every evening, and her old school friend was having an affair with a man and was hardly ever there. 'I have to lie to her mother who rings up most mornings. To begin with I said that she was having her hair done because it was cheaper if she went early, but her mother became suspicious and wanted the telephone number of the hairdressers', so I said that she was out jogging.' Clare was unlucky because the girls with whom she shared, having got their men, did not want to collect more so did not bother to entertain.

Prue, who also lived with two girls, told me that she did meet people; the flat always seemed to be full of them, but she simply did not know who the men were. 'They don't like it if you ask them a lot of questions,' she said.

Other girls have said that every man they met only wanted to sleep with them, or sometimes, sadly, that they didn't. Men retaliated by saying that girls were just looking for meal tickets or someone to show off to their friends. As one man put it, 'It's not that I think I'm all that marvellous, but I'm male and have a pocket book.'

Lucy came to London at the age of eighteen knowing nobody, and she was lucky to get a room in the YWCA. An efficient shorthand typist she managed to get a job. She worked during the day and learnt book-keeping in the evening. By the time she was twenty-four, this hard work had paid off financially and she was earning a good salary. Socially, though, it was a disaster; she had had no time to cultivate friends. She admitted to me that she envied the couple in the flat next to her who had terrible rows and shouted so loudly that she could hear every word they said.

Many girls, from all social strata, come to us because of their lack of social life. Big towns with their concentration of people are far more lonely than small villages where everybody has a place in society. In the towns it seems as if nobody wants to know, and as if everybody else is having a good time. People who are busy are not necessarily happy. Many have jobs which entail meeting a lot of people, but the difficulty lies in making your own small circle of friends from amongst all these people.

Carol was pretty, and showed her looks to their best advantage. She did not wear much make-up—she had good features and large eyes and didn't need it. Her skin was well cared for and so were her hands, and her hair was fashionably and very well cut. She wore expensive separates which I felt sure she would interchange well. She had spent a lot of money on her handbag and boots, and wore a very handsome gold chain. She said, 'Having spent the last six years as a career girl and prior to that travelled abroad, I feel it's time to settle down and share life with somebody else.' She had certainly travelled—across the Sahara and from there down to South Africa, and in India and South America—but the hard way, in jeeps or by public transport. In her present job as representative of a large dress-manufacturing company she had to travel, but in a 'more de luxe way', she said, which she found rather boring.

A girl of twenty-eight whose fiancé had married her best friend wrote: 'Now that I have stopped thinking every moment of the day of somebody whom I loved and can think of him with affection I consider myself ready for marriage.'

Mark seemed amiable but said he had no friends. He worked hard in a small office all day and then went back to his pad, a room with a Belling cooker, and a shared bathroom. He earned a good salary but saw no reason to spend it on better accommodation unless he had someone to share it with. He liked theatres and cinemas and often went to them alone, he talked well and intelligently about them. He was also well read. Rather to my surprise I saw from his form that he came from a large family. I asked if he got on well with them. He said that he did but they were pretty scattered. He had one brother in Australia, another in Canada, and a sister in South Africa. The rest of the family lived in the West Country and he went down for Christmas and special occasions. He was pretty self-sufficient but would like an extroverted wife who would make friends easily so that they could entertain.

116

Bill's trouble was that he was always moving round England. His firm had branches everywhere and as a management trainee it was necessary for him to be away from home a great deal in order to get to know them all. These continued absences had made his fiancée break off their engagement. She also suspected him of having girl friends in other towns. It was a situation which would have proved disastrous if they'd married.

Edward moved about from one continent to another as representative of an international firm. The representatives in the other countries were hospitable, almost too much so, sometimes arranging parties which he did not want to go to. He was given a large entertainment allowance and had to entertain them in return. As he said, he had acquaintances all over the world but no real friends. He intended to stay another two or three years in his present job and then find work where he could be at home. He would like a wife to come home to now, but one who would take an occasional business trip with him. Later he would like to have a settled home and travel only for pleasure.

A dishy radio interviewer who came to see us said, 'I meet interesting people all day; I have to give out to them to put them at their ease and to get them at their best. I love it, but sometimes I am talking with people for hours a day and at the end of it I am not only completely whacked, but have made acquaintanceships that are unlikely to turn into friendships.'

Many ambitious and highly trained men are leaving Britain because they find that the working conditions in other countries are better — but they still want British wives. One businessman whose activities were centred in Europe used to fly into London to give girls lunch. Once he met somebody whom he really liked he continued his courtship into dinner and possibly a theatre. Another man who lived in Malta used to fly to England every Friday and return late Sunday night. When he paid his after-marriage fee he laughed and said, 'The fee is practically the same amount as the air fare that I have been paying every week.'

Not all our clients are in these categories. Some of them live in or near big towns where they and their families have lived for generations, and where they have life-long friends. When they come to see us they say, 'The trouble is, I've never really met anybody I've wanted to marry.' Mary — pretty, vivacious, with large brown eyes — was one of these. 'I've always had a good time,' she said, 'but never really been in love with anybody and suddenly everybody I know seems to be tied up with somebody else.'

Gavin — who seemed to have a double row of jet black eyelashes about an inch long — said, 'I've had quite a lot of girl friends, but never felt serious about any of them. Now I would like to fall in love but cannot find anybody quite right for me.'

Most of the thirty to forty-year-olds who come to us have been married before and have children. Priscilla loved discos and night life generally, but said that her enjoyment was lessened when she added up the money that she would have to pay out to babysitters when she got home.

A more serious-minded woman said, 'Because I have very little scope [being at home] for meeting people, I'm increasingly aware of my own and the children's needs for a husband and father.'

If women who are single parents have jobs they suffer in the same way as men in a similar situation. Sometimes they find a gem who likes looking after children and seems happy in their home, but they can also be reduced to employing someone whom they hope is not as bad as she seems, because they cannot find anybody else. One woman who had two children of her own married a man with three and wrote me the following letter:

It is now over five years since our wedding day and we thought that you might like to know that we are happy (five children, cat and all). I would like you to know how wonderful it has been taking on three stepchildren. It may help others to consider this sort of situation and to know that it *can* be very rewarding and not all the hard work it might seem to be. For instance we have a friend whose wife died leaving him with two children. He would like to marry again but does not consider it fair to expect a woman to take on the whole family.

Mothers in their twenties and early thirties who have young children are often more difficult to cater for than older women whose children are in their teens and about to leave home. Several times recently men have said that they would not mind meeting young unmarried mothers, but not ones that had been divorced. When asked why, they have replied that they would find it easier to treat the child as their own than if it had a father with whom it went to stay for several months in the year and who would be making decisions about its education, etc.

Men and women in their thirties and forties come to us either because they have had unsatisfactory engagements or affairs, or because they have been part of a close little circle which has suddenly broken up; all the others seem to be getting married leaving them the odd man or woman out. Or else they have concentrated so much on their jobs that they have neglected their social life. In this age group 'bachelor' women are more difficult to find partners for than the men, as they do not have such a wide choice. Women are prepared to meet men up to ten years or so older than themselves, but older men usually want to meet a younger woman, or one who has been married before: they think she will be more amiable. The men in that age group can meet girls in their twenties; sometimes they are willing to meet women who are two or three years older than themselves, seldom more.

Women in their forties or fifties, if they have been

married before, have often led the sort of life which depended upon their husband's position. If he dies or they part they are very much alone and need help. It is not an easy age group because at this age there starts to be a shortage of eligible men. Some unmarried men in their fifties say that they are marrying because they want to have children. Sometimes this is simply an excuse to meet younger women; if it is not and they genuinely just want children I think they are incredibly selfish. They want a young woman first to nurse and bring up their children and then to nurse them in their old age.

From sixty upwards there are even fewer men: this is a statistical fact. Men die younger than women do and we find it difficult to help many of the women. We have, however, had some very happy and to us exciting older marriages. One couple were in their seventies, and strangely enough both had been married through us before. But the strangest case that I have ever had was years ago. A man who had been a family butler had lost his wife a few years before. He was eighty, could we help him? We wrote and told him that we had not got anybody at the moment but would let him know when we had. A few weeks afterwards a woman who was also eighty, had lost her husband and had been a cook, wrote to us. They both lived in the North of England, not very far from each other. I wrote and said that we would not charge them a registration fee, only an after-marriage fee if they met and married. They did, and for several years afterwards we used to get a little card from them on their wedding anniversary.

It is interesting how much during the forty years since I started, people, their ideas, and their circumstances have changed, but the end product is much the same. Now everybody has more freedom, and there are more places where they can meet. But everything is transitory. It is not easy to turn acquaintanceships into friendships. People too are very mobile. They do not just move from town to town but from one country or continent to another. Now, too, it is not only the men who are going abroad, many women are leaving Britain as well. As things are, the world for many people is becoming larger and often much lonelier; this makes them all the more anxious to find somebody to marry, and often they need help in doing so. The most practical approach we had was from a young man who, when asked why he had come to us, said: 'If I want a car I go to a garage. So if I want to get married I come to you.'

12 Marriage Bureaux in France and the USA

Experience joined to Common Sense
To mortals is a Providence.
MATTHEW GREEN

In August 1953 I had spent a fortnight in Monte Carlo and met a man who had convinced me that I should have an office in Paris. Muriel Segal and I had just written *Marriage is my Business*. It had been translated into French and was to be published by Pierre Horay in the autumn under the title *Un mariage par Jour*. I decided to see how the book went before I did anything about an office. Meantime, the man knew a number of people in Paris and said he would keep his eyes open for a suitable manageress.

The book went quite well and the man produced two women, one of whom, Juliette Marchal, I thought would be perfect. She came over to work in my office in London to learn how to interview. She could not speak much English, but Dorothy, who worked for me then, spoke fluent and good French, and mine was fluent though ghastly.

We decided to keep the name 'Marriage Bureau', as in London, deliberately retaining the English spelling of marriage, to underline the affiliation with the London office. We took an office at 1 bis, rue du Havre — near the Madeleine — and the telephone number was Europe 3403-4-5, which made me feel that the business was really acquiring an international flavour. It was on the third floor of the building and had a typical Parisian lift which you were only allowed to use going up and which spent a large part of its time stuck between floors.

The room we had taken was large and well furnished. It was shaped like a cheddar cheese, with two lots of windows. One looked down into the rue du Havre and the other looked over Boulevard Haussman opposite the Printemps.

It was just before the days when it became illegal for drivers of cars to blow their horns in the city so when we had the windows open the noise was deafening; and about twice a day there was a screaming of brakes followed by a loud crash, which in Paris usually means an accident, extraordinarily minor generally in relation to the amount of noise involved.

In France arranged marriages were still looked upon as sensible and it was quite customary for a man or woman, especially in the remote country districts, to ask their parish priest to find them a marriage partner. If the priest did not know of anybody, he would ask a priest from another parish, or in some cases advise them to get in touch with an *agence de mariage*. There were at that time a number of these operating in the large towns and in Paris. They advertised freely and one or two stipulated that their potential clients must have a reference from a notary or a priest before they would take them on. Several of them stated that they refused clients who had been through the divorce courts. One claimed to have been going for a hundred years.

From the first it was obvious that my French clients had an approach very different from that of my English ones. In England a girl will often say something like, 'Will you please put Miss Mary B. Smith on the envelope, because I have a sister who has the initial M in her name and I don't want her to open the letter.' In France family ties were then much stronger than they were here. The parents and relations, even remote aunts and distant cousins, took a deep interest in the matter and I felt perfectly certain that any letter we addressed to one of the family would be read and discussed by them all. Filling in the form at home, I was sure, would be a joint effort as well. Even the young men or women who had broken away from the country and were earning their own living in Paris or in other big towns had aunts or cousins who kept a friendly and watchful eye on them.

Solange was typical. She was brought into the office by her mother and her mother's best friend. 'Solange is very *timide*,' the mother said, and the two of them discussed with Juliette Marchal the sort of man they thought Solange should marry. Solange never said a word during the whole interview and appeared to be only mildly interested. When I tried to draw her away to my desk to see if I could get anything out of her, she looked suprised, and the only thing she would say was that she was looking forward to getting married and having her own home. Romance, apparently didn't enter into it.

Another woman came in with four daughters. 'Look at them well,' she said. 'They will have the same dowry and they are nice healthy girls. If you marry off the eldest you can have the rest in turn.'

The men usually came in by themselves, but one came with his mother who proceeded to say in front of him that she thought that as he had a weak character and very little initiative he should marry a determined and organising sort of girl. The mother went out and while she started to walk down the stairs, the son came back to collect his gloves. He said, breathlessly, 'I will telephone to make an appointment to see you another day. Take no notice of what my mother has said. I loathe domineering women.'

We had the form we used in England translated fairly closely although we had to make one or two changes. In England, if you know where a woman or man has been educated, it tells you a great deal about them. In France it does not, so on the form we asked instead what degree of education they had reached. For figure we put 'silhouette'. In England people write 'medium', 'slim', 'thin', etc, in answer to this. In France one gets a different kind of response: several clients wrote 'agreeable', 'distinguished', 'elegant', 'athletic' and such like.

When Britons tell us their interests they put down, for example, reading, dancing, music, animals, children — nearly always in that order, animals then children. They very seldom say that they would like their wives or husbands to be affectionate. French people hardly ever mention animals or children. They say things that sound rather odd to English ears like, 'I love my interior', and another woman said, 'I have a love above all for sport'. They also said they would like their partner to have 'much heart' and 'an affectionate tenderness', or 'affectionate seriousness'.

One of the greatest surprises to me, though, was the number of French men who wanted to meet English women. One was a marquis, a big landowner and a farmer who liked living in the country. He said that he knew England well and thought that English women adapted themselves much better to being wives of gentlemen farmers than French women. He wanted to meet what he called a 'natural English rose'; he did not like make-up. As he was in his sixties and did not want to marry a woman very much younger than himself it was not as easy as it might have been. Most roses need a few unnatural aids to remain so, especially when they get into their fifties, added to which he was a strict Roman Catholic so the rose had to be too, and of course she could not be divorced. He had been a widower for ten years. He had a lovely house about a hundred miles from Paris and suggested that I send him a rose or two over to stay. He relied on my judgement, he said. Eventually, I persuaded him that he must write some preliminary letters himself so that he could establish some form of acquaintanceship, and when he had done that I suggested that he should take a trip to London to meet the woman and, if they got on well together, invite her to visit him in return.

Another man who wanted an English wife was a member of a very well-known family. I interviewed him because he came in without an appointment when Juliette was out. He seemed amused at my bad French and very soon during the interview switched to his much better English. He was young and very good looking and wanted to know if we could find him a girl with long slim bone structure, who knew how to wear country clothes and full evening dress with perfect confidence.

Other French men gave a variety of reasons for wanting English wives:

'English girls look fresh and clean skinned even if they have been tramping in the rain.'

'They wear well, they keep their figures better than Latin women.'

'A well-dressed English woman can be very elegant indeed, as she can have an aristocratic air which no other woman can copy. American women seldom rise above looking rich and bourgeoise, and French women look chic rather than well bred.'

Others rhapsodised less but still wanted British girls.

'English, Welsh or Irish girls are more sweet in character than French.' (I never found out what he had against the Scottish.)

'English women bring up their children much better than we do.'

'I like English women and am quite prepared to teach one to dress properly.'

'I want a wife who will accompany me on my travels and will not be so domesticated that she will want to remain at home all the time.'

I had anticipated that French women would want to meet English men. One reason they gave was that they thought English men were more reliable; one woman described French men as 'very butterfly'. Others said such things as:

'English men are more considerate, I have heard they they even help with the washing-up.'

'I would like to live in a good climate in one of your colonies, if you have any left.'

A French girl who had been studying in England wanted to live in the country, which she said she loved. 'I like everything English except the food and London,' she wrote.

One French woman had three daughters. Her eldest had married an English man, she wanted the others to do likewise, because she said he was a reliable and considerate husband.

Juliette summed up some of their views in an interview with Olga Franklin, published in the *Daily Sketch*. 'French women do not think your men are cold. Quite the contrary — they are only cold to other women and that is why they make such splendid husbands. They are more faithful and reliable. Besides, French men demand a dowry and English men rarely ask for that.'

Very few English women joined the French office, although several of my London branch clients said that they would like to marry French men. One thought that French men were more appreciative than English men. One wanted to have a lot of children. 'French men,' she said, 'are more used to a large family than English men are, also they are more sympathetic, charming and easier to talk to.' Another said, 'They are much more houseproud and adaptable about the house.'

English men said French women were better companions and conversationalists, much more domesticated, and generally make more of an effort.

One wrote, 'What I like about French women is that they can go out for a walk or play golf and look as if they had been in a Beauty Salon all the afternoon.'

An English man said, 'They are the only truly feminine women left. They don't even want to be emancipated, they just want to rule their homes.'

The only dissenting voice was from an English man working in France who said, 'I definitely don't want to get caught up in the coils of a French woman. You'd always be trailing along behind, picking up dropped earrings and gew-gaws; and anxiously counting your money.'

Quite early on I began to think it was a matter of the grass being greener on the other side of the fence.

The most tiresome hanger-on we had at that time was an American, who said he could get an advertisement for us into the American Forces newspaper, published in France. Thinking he was a bona fide agent we were naturally keen on this. He was one of those bullet-headed clean-looking Americans who looked as though he lived on deodorants and mouth washes, and we felt he must be clean inside and out. Unfortunately he had nothing to do with any Forces magazine and was simply trying to find out how we were doing and if it would be possible to exploit us as a call-girl agency. We tumbled to this fairly soon, but it took several months before he gave up hope, and he used to bombard us with long telephone conversations and on the whole waste our time.

I stayed in Paris for three weeks helping Juliette and, as many of the clients wanted to see me personally, I took some of the interviews. In a funny way my atrocious French helped to put people at their ease. A man who eventually got married through us, wrote: 'Your French has improved every time I talk to you, if you would only remember a few simple rules of grammar and pronunciation you would speak quite well.'

A schoolmistress ticked me off in a letter when she wrote, 'When I spoke to you on the telephone this morning you were still confusing your past and present participles. I told you about that last time.'

After a few months away I took over from Juliette for another three weeks. She had worked very hard at great pressure and needed a holiday. She lent me her flat while she was away and told me that there would be no hot water as there was no one to stoke the boiler in the building. She also assured me that as it was July there would be 'nobody' in Paris—so I would have a nice easy time.

She was right about the hot water, but not about the nice easy time. By the end of each day I was positively reeling with fatigue, largely caused by trying to understand what people had written or said.

The telephone was the worst — Paris is notorious for having the rudest operators in the world, and a foreign voice seems to rouse their most savage instincts. It was in any case more difficiult for me to talk to somebody if I could not see them. Added to this I thought that I should interview as many of my clients as possible in their homes as with my limited knowledge of French educational standards, etc, it would help me to assess their backgrounds.

When an English person came into my office I was so delighted to be able to speak English that I welcomed him or her with a heartiness completely out of proportion to the occasion. Quite a number of my English clients who were on holiday called in out of curiosity. One of them who was bilingual was there when the telephone rang and I found myself in particular difficulty trying to take down a name and address. After a bit he could bear it no longer and seizing the telephone from me took down the address himself. Juliette had left me copies of standard letters but they did not always cover everything and as this client had been so obliging once or twice I telephoned him at his hotel to see if he could help me out, which he did.

By the time I left, one or two people seemed to be interested in each other, and a few weeks after I returned to England Juliette wrote, 'I have the joy of announcing the marriage of Monsieur Bernard and Mademoiselle Coupe.' This was confirmed the next week and she added, 'We have two more marriages approaching.'

The first actual marriage was between a man from the French Colonies who married a widow. He was so enthusiastic about our business that when he returned to his work he put an advertisement in the local paper for us. Solange followed rapidly. She got engaged to a nice young insurance agent, and seemed to take the whole thing as a matter of course.

Dorothy, my principal assistant in London, was my right hand in all this because she wrote French as well as she spoke it. Right at the beginning Juliette had written, 'Dorothy is an angel to aid me in all the things that I have demanded.' Dorothy was. But there was a certain amount of competition between the two and occasionally one tried to palm off on the other a client who was not suitable. 'Please tell Dorothy,' Juliette wrote to me, 'that Monsieur Jacques wishes to marry a *young* English girl.'

Dorothy kept her end up well. 'It is useless to expect any of our clients to want to meet such a very short Frenchman,' she wrote on one occasion; and on another, 'Madame Boucher makes great capital out of the fact that she can run a house. English women have to do that, too. Has she any other special qualifications?'

Juliette counter-attacked smartly, 'Can Major X. speak French, or will he just make signs when he comes over here.' She relented later though. 'If you have a man around sixty years, very distinguished, free — retired from his affairs, wishing to meet a French woman of fifty-eight years, very pretty, elegant, very rich and adoring travel, send me the introduction. She looks for a voyaging companion, a little snob and worldly enough.'

The romance that caused the most concern was that between the marquis and the English rose. Unfortunately, rather against my better judgement, I allowed Miss Matthews to meet him. She was in her forties, but liked older men and had already written to say she would like to meet any French clients whom we thought might be suitable. She had told us when she first came into the office that her family came from France and that their name centuries before had been Matthieu — despite this she spoke no French. She was an English rose though, and had such a beautiful skin and complexion that we felt the Marquis could not fault her on that count. The problem was that she was terribly refined in both speech and manner. Whether Monsieur le Marquis would notice or mind we were not quite certain. At last, however, we decided to try.

From then on things moved quickly. Thrilled because he had a title, and against our advice, she accepted his invitation to go over and stay with him. Despite my warnings he still sent these invitations, mainly to save himself the trouble of coming over to England, and we told her that he did so. But nothing would stop her and over she hurried.

Everything went wrong. The marquis—a stickler for propriety—had an unmarried sister who used to move into the house if he had a single woman to stay. He had explained this to Miss Matthews who was enchanted by his chivalrous instincts.

Unfortunately, at the last minute, the sister became ill and did not move in. Unfortunately too, Miss Matthews drank a bit too much wine at dinner and the whole affair ended by her slapping his face and barricading her door. He asked us indignantly, 'What did she want then, the way she behaved?'

After that there was a pause until we introduced him to a woman not quite so rose-like, but attractive and sensible, and with a good command of French. She also had the advantage of having relations in Paris and she stayed with them when she went over to meet him. A few months later they were married.

After eighteen months we closed the office in Paris. Juliette for private reasons was constantly having to go abroad and I had so many commitments in England that I could not spend enough time in Paris to fill in the gap, and it would not have been worth my while to neglect my business in England. In fact, as I had not had a business in France before the war, any money I earned there was frozen until everybody had had a go at taxing it, so the Paris Bureau was unlikely to be a financial success. I had known this before I started, but had not minded as I was eager to expand in any way I could and I love France. When Juliette had to leave, though, we could not find anybody suitable to take her place, so we had to call it off and over several months she handed over her clients to another reputable Paris bureau.

It had been an interesting experience and something of an education. I had learnt to appreciate the amazingly strong family feeling that existed in France and is still so much stronger than in Britain. I also began to understand their more practical, less romantic, approach to love and marriage. On several occasions I was told by both men and women that the English man was the most idealistic and romantic man in the world.

I had also had blown sky high for me a myth which had been instilled in me since childhood—that French women were the best dressed, best looking, best everything in the world, and the most admired. Like most nations they are a mixture. Their top-grade women, expensively dressed, made-up and perfumed, are hard to beat; but the British middle-income group, thanks to the availability of good medium-priced clothes and a new consciousness of make-up and grooming, can now hold their own very well with the French.

The other myth that was exploded for me concerned the French businessman and his attachment to work. I had often heard their jokes about the English weekend: English men leave on Friday evening and do not come back until Monday morning. I used to find in France that the men I wanted to get hold of for business reasons had left for the country on Thursday night and had not bothered with Monday at all because so many places in Paris are shut on that day. Often Wednesday would be a saint's day so the office would be closed then, too. This may be a slight exaggeration, but the English weekend, in my experience, takes far less of a slice out of the working week than does the French routine.

In 1973 Suzanne, a French woman journalist and the niece of a great friend of mine, wrote to me from Paris and suggested that she should start up another Bureau for me in

France. Since I had wound up the rue du Havre office I had been in Paris only occasionally, for a few days at a time, or on holiday, so I was out of touch with what was going on in the marriage business. I told her this and asked her to do some investigating before I came over to discuss the matter with her. When I arrived I found that she had been thorough. She had written in the guise of a possible client to several bureaux who had simply asked her to fill in a form and send the money, which she had not done. She had been interviewed at one much advertised bureau and paid a fee, which had been the equivalent of nearly £100 sterling. She was not given a receipt when she paid in cash.

As her family was well known in theatrical and artistic circles in France she used a false name, but otherwise she told the truth about herself, giving her correct age and salary and her private means. She had been very highly educated which she mentioned too and she gave her qualifications. She did not say that she was a journalist, but that she was a writer. For several weeks she heard nothing, then one Saturday evening she was asked to go to the office the next afternoon to meet a man who, she was told, was a horticulturist. Assuming he would be well educated and perhaps scientifically qualified she went along. There were ten women in the waiting room when she arrived and the man, who sat in a small office, had them sent in to him one by one. When it came to her turn they gaped at each other in amazement. He was the gardener of a great friend of hers whom she visited frequently. She said that she did not know which of them was the more embarrassed.

Sounding out the general opinion about marriage bureaux in Paris amongst her acquaintance, particularly those in the press, Suzanne found that they had acquired a bad reputation. If we started again we would have to advertise how strict we were and get publicity to that effect as well. Even then the Bureau might not stand much of a chance. Suzanne could not afford to give up her job and concentrate entirely on anything we started, and I with my many branches on this side of the Channel would not have time to keep going over to France. Also, I could visualize Suzanne leaving and me having to rush over to Paris to replace her. Reluctantly, we decided to abandon the idea for the time being.

In 1955 Stephen Potter and I were married and as he was going over to the United States to lecture I went with him. I wanted to see if I could be affiliated with any of their established marriage bureaux: I had always understood that they had had them for years.

Six months before we left I went to the American Embassy in London and looked up the marriage bureaux for New York City. The advertisements all came under the heading of Marriage Brokers. 'Open your hearts to love,' said one. And another, 'Sincere, confidential service. Single, widowed, divorced, all ages and religions, introduced to ideal life partners. Couples with own licences married immediately opposite Maceys.' A third ran, 'We arrange Dignified Appointments for Your Daughter Without Her Knowledge.'

Under the same heading were the advice bureaux. One was called simply 'Alimony Inc.' and said, 'We fight alimony, visitation, abuses.' Another one said, 'Healing marriages performed and problems adjusted.'

I picked out twelve brokers and wrote to them. In the letter I said who I was and asked if I could come and see them, as I was interested in expanding my business on a British-American basis. After a few months and no replies I wrote a second time and again there were no answers. As I had been brought up to believe that nobody is as prompt in answering letters as the British, I wasn't too worried about this and decided I would just call in when I got over there.

The first address I went to was in a shabby-looking downtown office block. I couldn't find any trace of the bureau's name on the board and when I appealed to the porter he told me that he had never heard of the company, although he had been there for two years.

The next place I tried called itself 'Miss X's'. The door was opened by a very tall man who, when I asked to see the proprietor, said rather crossly, 'I am Miss X.' I explained who I was and what I had come about and he reluctantly allowed me to come in. The office seemed to consist of two rooms, a waiting room and his office. He was alone, and there was only a small filing cabinet and no sign of a typewriter, or the usual office paraphernalia. This surprised me because this bureau had claimed in its advertisement that it had been going for forty years and also had printed in large letters 'COUPLES WITH OWN LICENCES MARRIED IMMEDIATELY'. Trade seemed remarkably slack.

Miss X said that he thought he remembered getting my letter but he did not apologise or give any reason for not answering it; he sat there apparently sunk in complete indifference. I got up, said goodbye and left. Miss X just managed to drag himself to the door but more I felt to make sure that I had really gone than as a gracious gesture.

Next I called at a bureau that had been much publicised. It claimed to have branches in seventeen cities and that the owner was the doyenne of all bureaux. Here again I drew a blank at the address given in the business directory, but the porter this time said that he thought they had moved either to San Francisco or to Chicago. I was going to San Francisco at the end of the week so decided to try there.

I telephoned the other bureaux to see if they were still functioning. Two answered and, giving a false name, I made appointments to call. At the first I said I was an English woman who would be staying in New York for some time, knew nobody, but would like to marry an American. I asked what the fees were, and was told that they would be fixed according to the difficulty of my case. Would I please fill in the form? I took one and said I would fill it in at home and would call in again with it later. At the next place the woman seemed really interested in the case I put before her. I said that I had come on behalf of my brother who was a titled gentleman and would be coming over to the States and would be in need of companionship. She was so pressing that she wanted to start communications with him at once — he would pay according to the number of introductions he had, she said. Both of these offices were like Miss X's, there was no sign of staff or office equipment.

The office in San Francisco was better equipped, it was large and well furnished and had at least one secretary and a manageress. The principal was not there but the manageress and I had a long talk together. She told me that they too had a sliding scale of fees. Women under thirty paid $100, those between thirty and forty-five $150, and those over forty-five $250. I said that I had tried their office in New York and she seemed surprised to hear that it was not functioning, but said that they had a Friendship Centre in a downtown hotel. The principal, she thought, must be in Chicago. I would find her address in the book if I went there.

The three marriage bureaux that I had penetrated, at least to the extent of talking to them, all called themselves Friendship or Social Centers as well as Marriage Bureaux. They did not say that they were for marriage only. Their forms all asked a great many questions. The clients had to list their favourite restaurant, night club, newspaper, magazine, columnist, radio commentator, radio columnist, disc jockey, cartoon strip and comedian. One asked how well did they remember people's names? Another asked if they smoked or had a social drink? Not one of them asked a single question about the person the client would like to meet.

Back in New York I went to the address of the Friendship Circle I had been told about in San Francisco. The man behind the desk said that they used to have regular meetings, but it was several years since they had done so.

The first time I encountered computer dating was in 1957 at San Diego University, which had been open for only three weeks. Stephen was the first person to lecture there. Having lunch in the university afterwards I learned that they were using a computer to get the social life of the several thousand students started. Students paid two dollars for a card on which they could indicate their particular interests, this was then fed into the machine. The aim was to bring together those with similar interests; they could then form clubs, baseball teams, literary societies, etc.

We went to America again at the end of the year to find that the idea had already become commercialised. Computer machines had progressed a stage further and were now advertising that they would find you the right partner. One was called Mate-o-matic. In theory if a girl from New Jersey wanted to meet a man with similar interests and tastes in Manhattan, who had a certain type of job and earned a certain income, all one had to do was to press the right button. I also read about such a machine in Hollywood. It was called Univac, and Art Linkletter used it in his NBC show, 'People are Funny'. The programme advertised for people who wanted to get married, and made the one thousand responders fill in a questionnaire about their personal lives and preferences. Out of these they chose a girl called Barbara and with the help of the machine they produced a suitable husband for her—John. When they were introduced they got on very well, they survived four shows in which they had to tackle word games and their winnings approached $20,000. After this they announced their engagement, but they crashed on the fifth show, salvaging only $1,000 and a trip to Paris. Then Barbara broke off the engagement.

One of the computers was reputed to have had the details of a gorilla fed into it which it produced as a fitting mate for some astonished girl. I would love to know what she had asked for. Strong? Silent? Hirsute?

I tracked down an office in New York which was advertising that it had a computer, but never found anyone there who could explain what the business was all about. The next

137

time I was in New York I visited another Introduction Service which said that it was computerised. In fact the machine was a tabulating machine and it was out of action. The director told me that it tabulated everything under various headings, age, religion, environment, etc, so that when they wanted to find anybody in a particular category it was impossible for any one of them to be missed out; the great advantage was that anybody could work the machine. This did not seem to me to be a very good point as 'anybody' could not or should not sort out the cards that the machine threw out.

The form they used was more complicated than ours but the first question was forthright — it asked 'With whom do you live?' The clients were then asked how many brothers and sisters they had; their parents' marital status (please check); their relationship with them; to which of them they were most similar (please check); and if their marriage was happy (please check) and to what degree. It then went on through the clients' education, occupation, religion etc, to the number of times they had been in love, engaged, or married; and progressed from personal habits, likes and dislikes, to whether they had been psychoanalysed and whether they liked or disliked animals.

Finally came the question I would have found most baffling of all. It was about their social status. No loose thinking was allowed. A tick had to be put against one of the following: upper class, lower upper, upper middle, middle, lower middle, upper lower, lower. I would have found it difficult to answer this one. I think I was born somewhere amongst the upper, but now I vary between upper lower and lower on the days when I have menial and boring tasks to do, and between upper and lower upper on days when they are all done for me. The director and I had a long talk together and for several years afterwards if anybody asked me for the name of a bureau in New York I gave them hers; she also sent me one or two clients. Then one would-be client reported back that she was no longer there, so that came to an end.

In the autumn of 1958 I went to New York by invitation. Three people there thought there would be a place for a marriage bureau run on the same lines as mine. One of the three was Adele, who had been on the personnel side of a large magazine before her marriage. Her husband, a publisher, was another and the third a man who was publicity director of a large TV company. Adele was interested in running the office and the men were going to deal with the business and publicity aspects, and help in an advisory capacity.

I was very excited about this because they were exactly the sort of people I wanted to be associated with in such a business and I was quite sure that there was room for a bureau in America.

During my many visits to the States I had seen several of my old clients, and I was confident that American-British marriages worked. One couple had settled there soon after the war. He was an engineer and one way or another had had a hard time getting going. By the time I saw them they were firmly on their feet and had a nice house and two delightful children. Another client of mine was expecting his bride from England and asked me if I would go round the apartment he was furnishing to see if I could suggest any English touches, so that she would not feel homesick.

Adele and I went through everything. We practised interviewing together. I told her how I dealt with difficult cases or situations, and explained our filing system in detail. Their solicitor drew up a simple contract between us and I was convinced that it was going to happen. Then, unfortunately, Adele decided it would be too much for her. She had not fully realised, although I had told her before I came over, that when we first started, Mary and I had worked a ten- or twelve-hour day. I had told Adele that I thought that it would be tougher still in New York and that she should get somebody to help her, possibly a partner. In my opinion all the so-called marriage bureaux I had visited in America had been

139

phoney — the only one I had thought genuine had been the Introduction Service. The manly Miss X. was probably running a call-girl service. The woman in New York who had told me that the fees would vary according to the difficulty of my case, and the woman in San Francisco who gave me a rising scale of fees for older women, would undoubtedly take on older women even if they had nobody for them. For the $250 quoted by the San Francisco woman for women over forty-five she could well afford to pay one, or even two, men $20 or so to take a client out and stand her a drink. A difficult case, meaning that the bureau has only a few introductions for a client, does not mean more work for the bureau, usually rather less, because there are not so many letters to write on the client's behalf. Adele would have not only had to live down the bad reputation that the American agencies had, but would have had to vet everything herself and work far harder than we had done when we first started.

In the mid-sixties several computer agencies started up in Britain. Some took space on a computer, running all the cards through once a month; one agency did this for twenty pounds a time. A reporter investigating·these agencies since then said that only two actually owned computers. John Patterson of Computer-Dating and Singles certainly does. He does not interview people and his forms are made out on the 'tick' theory. He is an enterprising man and caters chiefly for the young and adventurous who are not necessarily looking for a deep relationship.

Looking in the New York Telephone Directory recently I noted there were fewer marriage bureaux listed and only one of the marriage bureaux that had been advertising in the fifties was still there. It said that it had been going since 1920 and was for 'friendship, love and marriage' but I can't remember having come across it when I was in America.

In the current directory there are several computer and dating services with questionnaires designed by professional psychologists. These advertisements, together with those for the marriage bureaux, take up only one and a quarter columns, but four and a half columns are taken up by Marriage Counselling Services. In its advertisement one asks 1. Is your marriage worth saving? 2. If it is — are you willing to struggle to save it? 3. If your marriage is worth saving — what should you do? The answer is, of course, that you should consult the service. Probing into this a little I was told that some of the counselling services give good advice and that their counsellors are highly trained, but they are expensive. There is talk of having state advisory services in the same way as we do.

The British were ahead of the Americans by about forty years when the government-financed Marriage Guidance Council started. It has branches all over the country, trained counsellors, and the service is free. The law has changed over the years in Britain, making it much easier to get a divorce. The Americans became known for their multiple marriages and divorces years ago. Now they seem to be trying to put a brake on them. It will be interesting to see if they manage to do so, and if Britain will follow suit.

The fact is that each country has influenced the other. At the beginning of this century it was much easier to get a divorce in America than it was in Britain. Today there is not a great deal of difference although, of course, the law changes from state to state in America, whereas in Britain it is uniform throughout the country. Americans are inclined to like things more cut and dried than we do. In Britain husbands and wives are more likely to have long-standing affairs that are acknowledged by their spouses. This may of course be a habit left over from the more difficult divorce laws, but British history is full of allusions to extra-marital affairs and the bastards bred from them.

William the Conqueror, the first king to establish law and order in this country, was the bastard son of Robert who was the second son of Richard (The Good) of Normandy and Arlette, the daughter of a tanner. Henry VII was descended

141

from John of Gaunt and Katherine Swynford, whose children were only legitimised long after they had been born. His Tudor origins go back to the liaison of Queen Catherine, widow of Henry V, with a Welsh squire Owen Tudor. There is no evidence for their marriage, but the Tudors reigned all through the sixteenth century. Charles II made dukes of six of his illegitimate sons by various mistresses. The present Dukes of Grafton, Richmond and Gordon, and St Albans are descended from him.

The great families, too, had a code of their own. Once a wife had produced enough sons to ensure an heir — infant mortality was high — if her husband was liberal-minded and had his own paramours, she could have hers.

I asked one of my ex-clients, who had been a GI bride married through the Bureau and whom I visited in San Francisco, if she noticed many differences in the attitude to marriage in America. She agreed with me that if a couple fell for each other outside marriage they were more likely to get a divorce than their English equivalents who might simply go on having an affair for years. She thought that her husband was occasionally unfaithful to her — usually on business trips when girls were, or could be, provided. She had been unfaithful to him once or twice but it had never been serious.

Another of my clients, who had married a rich man and was living in New York, patted her blue rinse and, looking at her enormous solitaire diamond ring, said, 'Oh, he's got a floozy all right, but I doubt if he'd let it become serious, the alimony would be too much.' This is becoming the case in Britain.

During and after the war we had a great many American-British marriages. We do not have so many now and the pattern seems to be that American men want European wives and European women want American husbands, rather than the other way about. The older American women are exceptions. They say frankly that older men, or any men, are like gold dust in New York, and that they cannot compete with the man-hunting hostesses. 'They're ruthless, my dear,' one of them said to me. 'It's frightening. And with [here she mentioned the name of the ex-wife of a famous film star] on the hunt, nobody in her age group has a hope.'

Unfortunately I have to tell these American women that it is much the same in Britain where, although the hostesses may not be so ruthless, elderly men are at a premium too.

13 Running the Bureau

*My greatest thrill has been surviving
my imitators.*

WALTER WINCHELL

Of prime importance in running the Bureau is that people
know how to get in touch with us. When Mary Oliver and I
were painting that first office and my friend arrived and
suggested we telephone the newspapers I had been alarmed
and had strongly opposed the idea, but being unable to
back up my feelings I had given in. The reason for my
reluctance was that when I was eight, one of my cousins was
kidnapped. The cousin was rescued, and returned
unharmed, but my family were horrified by the publicity;
and I was imbued with the idea that it was, at all costs, to be
avoided. The newspapers had not, I found out later,
distorted any of the facts to do with the case, or done any
harm, but the idea had stuck. For this reason I hardly spoke
when the press came to see us at the Bureau. Luckily Mary
was splendid. She liked them and they liked her, and they
were extremely good to us. Gradually I got over my fears
and grew to like them too, and not only have I always found
them trustworthy and generous, but now I count many
journalists among my greatest friends. Despite a few early
and terrifying experiences on radio and television I enjoy
these, too. The technique of interviewing has much
improved over the years. Interviews are conducted by
questions and answers and one is so soothed by the lack of
tension and instruction that I always feel that if I passed out
cold they would cover up the fact and go on talking as if
nothing had happened.

Once the war got going we had a lean time: the impetus
of our initial publicity waned and newspapers were small

and full of more important things than us. I remember that at one time we were down to eleven pence in the bank.

In opposing the idea of publicity I had argued that advertising would be sufficient, and it had never occurred to me that after all our care to set up a genuine and respectable business the papers would not accept our advertisements. In the advertising managers' eyes we were associated with those seductive advertisements which we were fighting against. So, although our advertisement was short — 'The Marriage Bureau. Heather Jenner and Mary Oliver', followed by the address, telephone number and business hours — the prestige papers would not take us. The advertising manager of one famous national paper said that he would put us in if we could get a bachelor friend of his married. We did, but he did not keep his word. It was against the policy of the paper and he had not expected us to be successful.

We met the head of the Advertising Association. He said that he had nothing against our Bureau, but readers of the newspapers we wanted to be in would not like it. To be fair I saw what he meant. I had not told my family that I was starting the Marriage Bureau because I thought they would try and stop me: not because of the way we were working but because of the bad name that such bureaux had acquired on account of their seductive advertisements. One such advertisement might run as follows: 'Model, beautiful, good dress sense, well spoken, and fond of cooking. Could share with reliable gentleman.' Or, 'Ravishing-looking young divorcee, beautiful waist-length hair, would like to meet presentable gentleman fond of good living and travel.' These could be suited by the 'Successful Businessman. Six foot tall', who was married and would now like to share his life with a 'smart young lady'.

Such advertisements are usually put in by an agency. The genuine advertiser pays the agency, and anybody who answers also has to pay the agency in order to obtain the

145

name and address. In 1955 a charitable organisation which was investigating loneliness invited me to give evidence, and said that it could not understand why middle-aged women were so lonely when so many middle-aged men advertised in papers. I explained that the men would get twenty answers each, probably more, and that many of them had been put in by agencies playing the market.

After the war when newsprint was still short our first advertisements were in theatre programmes. The *Tatler* put us in and so did *Britannia* and *Eve*. Other magazines followed. The nationals were not interested.

Then several things happened. A London evening paper which had refused us began taking advertisements for escort bureaux. One ran 'Escorts for your evening out'. I wrote to the paper and asked that if it wouldn't take our straight advertisement would it put us in under 'The Marriage Bureau will provide you with permanent partners for your evenings in'. It wouldn't. A few years later the editors changed their minds and I put our usual advert in a few times, but I did not like the company I was keeping in their columns, nor did I get replies from the sort of people whom I would have taken on. The paper does not advertise escort bureaux now, but does advertise massage by beautiful girls, mixed sauna, and pregnancy testing. Its personal column is small—one advert said, 'André please return my clothes for Michelle's sake.' It sounded like the plot of a French farce.

In the sixties I wrote a column three times a week for the *Evening News* called 'Heather Jenner says'. I was never allowed to mention sex or the Marriage Bureau. It was only years after I had stopped writing for them that they said that they would take my advertisement.

Then a prestige daily paper took escort advertisements. This was really too much. I wrote to the advertising manager without success. Finally Stephen took a hand and wrote the following letter to the editor for me which I signed.

146

I am writing to you about a small matter which though seemingly trivial yet concerns me deeply and in a way may concern the reputation of your newspaper for fairness and just dealing.

On the surface it is not more than the question of acceptance or non-acceptance of an advertisement.

Twenty-nine years ago I found that the name 'Marriage Bureau' had a bad reputation in this country. It suggested 'lonely hearts clubs,' and get-together societies — devices for dating. Your paper felt the same about them and rightly refused their advertisements. During these years I have worked to transform the 'Image' of a Bureau into something which under my management has worked beneficially and specifically for *marriage*.

The work that I have done has been generously recorded by your paper in a full feature in your pages on May 17th 1966.

Is it not therefore wrong and misleading that my now famous Bond Street Marriage Bureau should have my restrained and factual advertisement refused place in your columns? This is an inconvenience. What is serious is that you are at the same time accepting advertisements for organisations which our experience tells us are a replica of those organisations which we have sought to discourage.

I am not of course complaining of your advertising manager to whom I have sent a copy of this letter. He had treated me with courtesy and according to his instructions. I do feel that these instructions need re-interpretation in the light of the facts.

Needless to say we were in — but then, Stephen even used to manage to get charming letters back from the Income Tax people. Since that time all the prestige papers take my advertisement. So, too, do the big provincial ones, although I have had a long battle with some of them, and there are still a few small local papers which do not.

It is said that imitation is the sincerest form of flattery, but I have found it tiresome as I have been copied so often and so badly. If I had invented a car or a knitting machine or some such thing I could have patented the name, but you cannot patent two common nouns, 'Marriage' and 'Bureau', we could only form a registered company, which we did on 26 June 1939.

In 1977 a briefing note was sent to me headed 'Advice To Prospective Patrons Of Marriage Bureaux And Dating Agencies'. The Director of Fair Trading, Mr Gordon Borrie, and I appeared on BBC and LBC radios and I said that I thought that the briefing note was perfectly fair, and I explained that many businesses who called themselves marriage agencies were no such thing. When the representative from Fair Trading had visited me I had told them how we worked and given them all our forms. I also said that many agencies put the word 'marriage' in their advertisement although they took on people who were not free to marry. I pointed out too that a real marriage bureau would not call itself a friendship bureau as well, and explained that it was people seeking the deeper relationship who would get hurt, if they fell in love with another member who said that they had joined merely for friendship.

I agreed that it would be a good idea to try to sort ourselves out and form an association. It would have to be an umbrella one to cover everybody mentioned in their note.

I went to various meetings, and finally John Patterson of Computer-Dating and I got together and drew up a suggested set of rules. At the start we said, 'The responsibility of marriage bureaux towards their clients is greater than those of other forms of introduction.' We had stricter rules for them: amongst other things, we said they should accept only people free to marry, should not send out lists of clients, or advertise them, and should not take on applicants who had not been interviewed by them.

We wrote to all the agencies whose names we could find and I asked my outside interviewers to look in the local press and give me any names and addresses from there. We found fifty-three. Forms from agencies who claimed to be marriage bureaux and who answered our letters were sent to me. Several of them, I found, sent different forms to their potential clients from the ones they sent to me and charged prices which varied from case to case. Generally, they left a space where the fee to be charged could be written in by hand rather than printed. Some self-styled marriage bureaux send out descriptions of people under age groups and reassuringly tell the clients that they will be put on the list when they join. These, and others, also took on people who were separated or still in the process of getting a divorce.

I went to a meeting with a group who wanted to come under the Marriage Bureaux heading but were not prepared to keep the rules. One had 'Dating' written on its notice board in the street. They wanted to be classed as a marriage bureau simply because they wanted to cash in on every relationship. They said that our rules would penalise them.

After that meeting I wrote to John Patterson and said that it was no use, I was not prepared to lower my standards to belong to an association. So Katherine Allen—who had always kept away from meetings—and I decided to form our own association which we would call the Society of Marriage Bureaux. We both keep the rules about which Counsel had advised me in 1939, and we have added one or two more. We sent a letter to the principal newspapers and magazines telling them what we were doing and advertised for any other genuine marriage bureaux to join us. Only three people wrote to us and we never heard from them again once we had sent them the rules.

Many papers who take or refuse our advertisements do not discriminate between their advertisers. The *Daily*

Telegraph, before they accept advertisements, ask to see a copy of the literature sent to the inquirers and a copy of the conditions imposed on clients by the Bureau. They also want to see an interview form, a specimen record card (if any), and to know the scale of fees charged. As well as this they ask pertinent questions about whether clients are interviewed or not, and whether the Bureau only takes on people who are free to marry.

This seems to be fair and sensible. The papers that write and say that if they take my advertisement they will have to take everybody else's are being absurd. If they advertise an hotel they don't have to advertise a brothel.

Once I have the clients, either through recommendation, publicity or advertising, it is very important that I have the right interviewers. The first interviewer whom Mary and I engaged and trained left us to become a Wren. Not long before she left I met Picot Schooling, who had been a casting director for a well-known theatrical agency. She was a friend of a great friend of mine and wanted a job. She was past calling-up age, which was what we were looking for, so we took her on. Mary then sold her share of the Bureau to me so Picot brought in Dorothy Harbottle, an old friend of hers, to be a secretary.

I was married by this time and living in Scotland but I came down for about a week once a month. Picot sent me copies of the forms of all the people who joined, along with her remarks about them, and we continued this practice of keeping duplicates out of the office because of the fire risk. During my weeks in London we went into it all more thoroughly and I did quite a lot of the paper work, the introductions, and answers to letters. I kept the books and paid the wages and bills from Scotland. Some of Picot's letters were short and to the point.

Mr Jones said he was bald through an explosion, but would not enlarge on it. Miss Fraser is very nice, rather fat, but has a lovely skin and teeth, and will inherit at least £30,000 from her father. She is interested in shooting, fishing, sailing, and politics (Conservative). She has a lot of personality and I should think would produce very healthy babies and wants to. She is an only child and I have introduced her to Mr Packer, but I think that you might like her for your Captain Allen. Cynthia Corbett isn't marrying after all—isn't she a Madam. (This was the second time that Cynthia had broken off the engagement.)

The lure of the stage called Picot back after the war ended. We came down from Scotland to live in Kent so I was commuting regularly and Dorothy took over as joint head with a friend of mine. Dorothy was quiet, gentle, and very loyal; and I don't think that I ever heard her make a nasty remark about anybody. As she had been my secretary, she still insisted on doing certain things for me when she became head. She had beautiful manners and with the confidence of her age group and upbringing always got what she wanted. If I wanted tickets for a theatre I would hear her say on the telephone, 'Miss Jenner never sits further back than the fourth row of the stalls, and likes to be in the middle.' And that was where I sat.

With the clients she was marvellous and very positive. If she thought that somebody was asking for too much she would tell them so politely but firmly.

One well-dressed and well-pleased-with-himself man coming in to her was what we would now call a chauvinist pig. When describing the sort of person he would like to meet he said that his wife would have to be good looking, well turned out, domesticated, fond of gardening and of living in the country—he actually lived in the suburbs. Dorothy asked him if he liked an occasional evening in London at a theatre and dinner afterwards perhaps, but he said no, he couldn't get out of the place fast enough. She asked him what he did about holidays, and was told that he always went off sailing, which he also did every weekend, and in the summer, when it was light enough, often in the evenings too. Dorothy told him that he was too selfish a man to make a good husband. She supposed that as he was forty and a bachelor he had got set in his ways and that he had better think a bit more about this and then perhaps come back again. Instead of being cross — it was evident from his attitude at first that he considered himself the catch of the season — he was apologetic. He simply hadn't thought of it that way. A few weeks later he returned. Of course if his wife wanted to go to a theatre he'd take her, and they could take it in turns to choose what sort of holiday they should have; if she liked sailing, too, it would probably be a good thing.

Another time a woman came in who had divorced her husband because he had run off with another woman. She was full of self-pity and had obviously let herself go. She had decided that the world was against her and she was a complete misery. Dorothy gave her a polite but firm ticking off. Other people's husbands had left them; anyhow, as she looked now who would want to marry her? She told her that before she would take her on she must pull herself together. She took the advice to heart and did just that.

The only fault I had to find with Dorothy was that she was not only a chain smoker and scattered ash everywhere, but she had a smoker's-cum-bronchial cough. One day when this was really getting on my nerves I very nearly said to her, 'You shouldn't smoke so much it's bad for you.' I then reflected that she must be getting on for eighty, and apart from her cough seemed to be in the best of health.

My younger interviewers and my daughter Stella adored her. She always had a twinkle in her eye and was a very good judge of character. After she retired in 1961 we all used to go and see her in her small smoke-filled flat in Cliveden Place. My last memory of her was at a party that Stella gave in 1965. Dorothy was sitting on a sofa with a gin and tonic and, of course, a cigarette. Gathered around her were most of the youth and beauty. I had to leave early, but Stella told me the next day that she stayed until nearly the last and continued in her quiet way to be the centre of attraction.

After Dorothy left, Evelyn, who had joined us in 1952, took over. By this time we had a staff of five interviewers. I had given up trying to have a personal secretary. If I found a good one she would want to become an interviewer after a few months. So I developed another system whereby every interviewer did some office work as well as interviewing, although looking after their clients was their most important job.

All my first interviewers had come into the office as secretaries and grown into the job. When publicity got going again and I was on the way to winning the advertising battle, I needed more staff, who had to be trained. I am fortunate in that quite a number of people write to me to say that they would like to work for me: if I need more I advertise. I see applicants myself and if I like them I take them into the main office, offer them coffee and we all sit and talk for a bit. When they leave I then ask the office their impressions. What we are looking for is somebody who looks pleasant, has a good manner, and who is not shy but is easy to get on with. They must, of course, have good references and be discreet. I like them to have dealt with people in some capacity in their previous jobs, but do not like the do-gooder. My clients are not in need of that sort of help: they want to talk to somebody with common sense and worldly knowledge who is approachable.

Having decided on a possible interviewer we train them in the office. First we ask them to look at the forms of the clients who have appointments that day and to make notes of the points which they would like the clients to enlarge upon. We then explain to any client who is going to be interviewed that we are training somebody and ask them if they would mind if they sat in. Most clients are agreeable to this. The trainee is told that she is not to speak, just to listen. After the

153

interview is over we ask her to assess the client and then we ask her to pick out from amongst our cards people whom she thinks would be suitable.

Some new interviewers are eager to interview on their own almost at once; they know that we are next door and can help them if they are in difficulty. Some are more diffident. One who eventually turned out to be one of the best interviewers I'd ever had and whom we all liked never asked to interview. So one morning I threw her in at the deep end when a client came in. Nervously she went out as if I'd asked her to detonate a time bomb, but after three quarters of an hour came back looking radiant. He was such a nice man and so easy to talk to. After that she never looked back.

The clients of course do not meet only the people who have been seen by their own interviewers. Behind the scenes in the office there is a certain amount of 'Do you think your Miss X would like to meet my Mr Y?' going on. The interviewers have to play fair and ask if they can use each other's clients. For instance, if we have a very beautiful girl or dishy man, for whom all our interviewers have somebody who would be interested, the person who is actually in charge of that client will decide whom she thinks is the most suitable, and can give or withhold her permission.

Evelyn reached retirement age in 1968 and then worked half time for us until my daughter Stella took over in April 1969. Stella had worked in the office before and left to get more experience on the understanding that she would come back as head or joint head with Evelyn. Joyce, a friend of Dorothy's niece who had also worked for us, was second in command. When Joyce first started she was supporting and looking after two young children on her own so could come to the office only a few hours a week, but she used to type my articles, and a book I wrote, from tapes at home. Once her children were old enough to stay at school all day she became an interviewer, and under Stella was a great help until she remarried.

Stella's authority was challenged immediately. I had two other young girls working in the office. One was able and conscientious and stayed with me for several years until she married; the other always behaved beautifully when I was in the office; worked well and was obliging. What I did not know was that when I was not there not only did she not pull her weight, but she often went home early, and was sometimes extremely rude to the rest of the staff. She tried her tricks on Stella at once, and the rest of the office watched. For three days Stella took no notice, but on the fourth she called the girl into the interviewing room and reduced her to tears. When she came out mopping her eyes she asked pathetically, 'May I go home?' 'No,' said Stella, 'get on with your work.' Mercifully she left a few weeks later.

Stella stayed with us until 1973 when she got married herself. She now has a child and does no work with the Marriage Bureau though she has typed this book for me. She was a very good head. She likes responsibility, keeps calm, and has an amazing memory. She could not only remember the names and addresses of her own clients, but also many of those belonging to the rest of us.

She sometimes had some odd experiences. One day she interviewed a woman who claimed that she had been a great friend of mine. The woman told her what school I had been to, that I had lived in Ceylon, and various other things. Stella wondered why, if she was such a great friend, she had never heard of her. She was also getting bored with hearing about me and wanted to hear about the woman, so at an appropriate point in my life story she said, 'And then she married my father.'

While she was working for me she was once or twice interviewed by the press. One reporter asked a great many questions: Why did people come to us, especially young men? Did we get a lot of rich men? Fortune hunters? Obvious neurotics? Stella answered them all very well when suddenly she was thrown a really difficult one. 'What would you do if a homosexual came to you and said that he wanted a male wife?'

'Ask Mummy,' she replied with perfect composure. (The answer, if anybody is interested, is that we could not do anything because we only deal in legal marriages, and it is not the law of the land for two men to marry.)

Before Stella came I had a number of younger staff. Sometimes I called them the beauty chorus and sometimes the crazy gang. All of them were very pretty. The first one who applied to be an interviewer was only in her early twenties and I thought her far too young. Then it occurred to me that I had started the business when I was twenty-five and that my reaction was simply one of old age. She was so good that I took on more. At one time I had eight in the office and found that the young girls worked well with the older staff. They had the interests of their clients at heart, and were liked by them. They bought themselves wedding rings at Woolworths and called themselves Mrs to deter any of the male clients who might get ideas. In fact, any interviewer who is single is told that she can be a client if she chooses, but she must be given introductions in the normal way by other interviewers and the whole matter must be above aboard. Several of my interviewers have married through the Bureau in this way. I called my beauty chorus the crazy gang only when they were high spirited and played tricks on each other. They were very serious over their work.

As I use the name Jenner for business naturally enough many people do not know either my real married name or my maiden one. A woman who had been at school with me, but in the top form when I arrived as a junior at the age of eleven, had strangely become three years younger than I was. Another time Anne, who interviewed for me for several years, discovered that one of our clients who frequently visited us was a friend of her parents and often went to dinner with them. She had not seen him for years but they had a large picture of her in the drawing room and she was always in terror lest she should run into him on the stairs or in the waiting room. The father of one of my interviewers was a friend of mine and on the books. I kept his name off the files and looked after him myself. After he married he said, 'Elizabeth must be frightfully dumb if she doesn't twig how we met.' She never did.

One weekend when I was staying with some friends I had the most curious time. They had asked some people to dinner and one of the men turned out to be a client. I had not interviewed him but recognised the name. After dinner we played bridge and he was my partner. While he was dealing, my hostess, by way of making conversation, told him what my business was. He misdealt and dropped a card, retrieving which could have accounted for his flushed face. His concentration left him though, and my hostess remarked the next day that he couldn't have been well as she'd never known him play so badly.

Most people are shy about coming to the Marriage Bureau and do not want to broadcast the fact. When they telephone for details they often ask if we send the information in a plain envelope; they are reassured when we tell them that the business is private and confidential, which is printed on our writing paper and forms. Somehow, coming to us and asking us to find them somebody to marry is different from the other accepted ways of meeting people, and they almost invariably keep the fact secret. Because we are not alone in the office we are fairly well protected from embarrassing situations. In the case of the woman who had been at school with me I had kept out of the way. It is only if clients drop in without an appointment that we might inadvertently upset them. They are not so shy, however, as not to tell their children about us. Quite a number of our clients are sent by their parents who were our clients, and in the late eighties it should be possible in turn to see a grandchild, which would be very gratifying.

In the 1960s the whole structure of the Bureau changed. I

had started going out to the big towns with my lectures, and
as a follow up advertised that I or one of my interviewers
would pay regular visits to the area. Then a much better
idea was presented to me. A woman who lived in Edinburgh
had a son at the prep school where one of my stepsons was
teaching; through him she contacted me and suggested that
she work for me in Scotland. After she had trained with us
in London the Scottish branch started. A few months later,
Renée came into the office. She had read about the Scottish
branch in *Nova* and came to see if she could interview for
me in Bristol, which she did very successfully for two years.
Then her husband had to move to London because of his
work so she handed over the Bristol clients to a friend who
also came to London for training. Renée has been working
for me ever since in the Bond Street office. I started up more
outside branches. The Birmingham interivewer was a
woman whom I had known in Ceylon, and the Kent one was
at school with me. Four branches have been run by people
who have been married through the Bureau. I now have
fifteen interviewers throughout the country.

All my outside interviewers work from home on a
commission and expenses basis. It is a perfect job for a
woman who is interested in marriage, has worked with
people before, and is good with paper work, but has
domestic ties. For the most part they all interview in their
own homes, but will meet clients outside if they can arrange
it. They are all trained by us and if they come to London
call in at the office. I travel round and see them regularly in
their own districts, usually about once a year. They can, of
course, always get in touch with us, and my visiting stops
them feeling out on a limb. When I am there they can talk
over any problems or ideas they have. They also contact
each other. If, for instance, my Yorkshire interviewer needs
help with introductions for a client, she can get in touch
with Tyneside or Birmingham, and of course London. Some
county clients, usually because they are well known in their

own area, prefer to deal with London direct anyway. It is their choice, and one of the reasons for having local branches and outside interviewers is to make it more convenient for the client. Another advantage is that the interviewer will know more about the area than we would in Bond Street.

Interviewing at home is less formal and some of our clients look upon the outside interviewers as mother confessors. Also, as they do not keep to office hours, their clients may telephone them in the evenings, particularly if they are feeling lonely. One Christmas Eve a man who was on the books felt sad and left out of things and telephoned one of the interviewers. She was so sorry for him that she asked him to Christmas lunch. Her husband was furious, but she said he was a nice man and that they were a man short. It turned out better than she had expected, except that she did herself out of her own commission. He married her cousin who had been the odd woman out.

In the North Country one of my interviewers who was a widow was going through the form with a man who had a fairly common surname when suddenly she asked him if he'd been at a certain kindergarten school. He looked at her in surprise and a broad smile came over his face, 'You're X.,' he said. She gave him several introductions, but after a few he proposed to her and they got married.

Having these branches means that we do not need such a large staff in London, and I now have only four besides myself. So far, with a few exceptions, I have been lucky with my interviewers. It is an interesting job for the right person, and they all find it enormously satisfying when their clients get married.

Renée has been with me the longest now, two years in Bristol and ten in London. Having been an outside interviewer herself she understands their problems. She is the quickest worker I have ever met and composes marvellous letters. They seem to fall from her typewriter like leaves:

some of them congratulatory, some conciliatory, and some reproachful or firm. She also looks after the advertising accounts, making sure that we are in the right papers on the right days with the right telephone numbers and addresses. These advertisements are in papers all over the country. She has a great sense of fun and is kind and ever ready to help, a very good interviewer, tactful, and much liked by her clients—a tower of strength in fact. I have a good team, ranging from the youngest in her late twenties, married and with children, to my age. Besides looking after our own clients the London office is the hub of the business. We send out to the various districts the inquiries that come in for people in a particular area, help sort out problems, keep everybody supplied with stationery, and generally make sure the wheels turn smoothly.

The marriage rate fell by two per cent in 1976—the last year for which the figures are available at the time of writing. This I think was caused chiefly by the low birthrate in the fifties. Births fell from 881,026 in 1947 to 557,811 in 1955, which means that today there are fewer people between the ages of 23 and 31, the age group in which most people make their first marriage. The numbers rose to 875,972 in 1964 so I would think that in the eighties the marriage rate will rise again. Amongst them I hope will be 'our grandchildren'.

The last forty years have been a rewarding time from a personal point of view. Apart from getting thousands of couples married and having happy and grateful letters from them, I have met and talked to people from all walks of life, not only about marriage but about ways of living, joys, sorrows and fears. I have in some way entered into their lives for which I consider myself lucky.

But I do not escape criticism. I have sometimes been asked if I think that I should take money from people who need help to get married. They imply that my clients are in extremes of distress and possibly poverty stricken. The short answer is that I never started out to be a do-gooder. I earn my living as do clergymen, doctors, people working for the social services, etc; and my clients are perfectly normal people. I have also always kept my fees as low as I can. In 1939 my registration fee was five guineas and the after-marriage fee ten guineas. Now the fees are £35 and £70 respectively, plus eight per cent VAT. Not many businesses have managed to keep their prices down in these proportions.

I am also accused of not taking on older women. I take on as many as I can, and warn them that they cannot have many introductions. The sad fact is that in the over-sixties age group there are two million more women than men.

As I have been going so long I am often asked if I will retire. I hope not. If you start something as individual and satisfying as I have, and if you are lucky enough to have good health and vitality, you just love it. I do not think that I would have had such a satisfying time in any other profession. The Marriage Bureau has been all-absorbing and is an integral part of my life.